CHALLENGE AND COURAGE:

GROWING THE FIRST COLLEGE PREPARATORY

HIGH SCHOOL IN LIBERIA

BY DR. SEI BUOR

I dedicate this book to Christian Leadership Training International and Riverview International Christian Academy ministry partners:

- ❖ Northwest Covenant Church, IL

- ❖ Glory To God Church Ministry, FL

- ❖ Santa Barbara Community Church, CA

- ❖ Foundation Church, CO

- ❖ Mission Resource International, IN

- ❖ tSOAR Discipleship Ministry, IN

Each of you has contributed and offered us your generosity, allowing us to develop God's Kingdom in Liberia. I am eternally grateful to God for your partnership, which has amplified our influence and ability to restore hope and to inspire a new generation of Christ-followers and nation-builders.

CHALLENGE AND COURAGE:

Growing the First College Preparatory High School in Liberia

By Dr. Sei Buor

Contents

Acknowledgments

I am deeply grateful to my dear wife, Yah Gbalalay Buor. In our 46 years of marriage, she always sends me out day after day with love, prayers and trust so I can do the work that God has called us to do. We have so many friends and family members in the fight of faith who are investing in our lives and ministries, and she wants to ensure all of them win. I LOVE YOU, YAH!

Special thanks to my dear friends Mark and Nicole Oehler for your incredible encouragement, financial generosity, and ever-present friendship and kindness in helping me write my third book. Mark has helped validate and fine-tune all of my works immeasurably beyond my creativity and imagination.

Sally Rushmore isn't just an editor-extraordinaire. She is also a fun person, and often delivers her critical comments and feedback while still making me laugh. Sally managed my first two book projects and now this project. Thanks for your help throughout the writing process, from first draft to finishing touches! I am exceedingly glad we reconnected on this project.

I also want to thank Mr. Jon Lieberman, my long-term friend and partner in the ministry. From the very day we met at a Grace Church-sponsored Global Leadership Conference in Noblesville, Indiana, in 2002, and throughout our project years, he has recognized the significance of my vision and has given me ongoing encouragement and support. Jon gave us insightful editorial support. He read through the first draft of the entire manuscript, sharpened my theological perspectives, and made invaluable suggestions.

In early 2002, the tSOAR group of Bill Ellison, Mark Oehler, Joe Williamson, and Duane Brooks provided me the initial encouragement that gave me an awareness of the power of my  own life stories, dreams and vision. These stories would give me a framework for helping to rebuild a country torn apart by 15 years of civil war. I was also part of a weekly men's Bible study with Brad Elliott, Don Litwiler, Jay Skinner, Dan Farrell. These men and others who cycled through these two groups were dear friends and they encouraged me to write my first book No More War: Rebuilding Liberia through Faith, Determination & Education, and later the second book Visions, Valleys & Victories: Growing Liberia International Christian College. These innumerable colleagues and partners have added to this body of work and its distribution over the years. I must give special thanks to each of you!

We're overwhelmingly grateful to our dynamic CLTI and RICA team members who are working in so many ways to serve our donors who have given generously so we can equip our students for sustained life change. To all, I say thank you and congratulations for a job well done!

Lastly, thank you to those who are reading this book. Thanks for believing in yourself and your God-sized dreams and visions. God created you and me to dream big. Dreaming will develop your faith and help you become the kind of person God intended you to be. So, I urge you to dream, and in your dreaming, be courageous!

Introduction

This book is written to explain the vision and tell the story of the foundation and development of Christian Leadership Training International (CLTI). It also expresses a deep appreciation to those individuals and churches that helped us. We believe the book's message will inspire others, as God leads them, to join us in this great adventure of teaching students and developing Liberia's future leaders.

I also am writing to challenge and encourage another audience of people. This group includes two types of leaders. The first ones are *young* visionary leaders who are just embarking on their journey to follow God. They will benefit from the teaching and experience of others. The members of the second group are more seasoned leaders. These are individuals who, based on various stages of their life when facing new challenges, still encounter deep disappointments. They may be rethinking their calling/career or considering launching out in a whole new direction in life. They are virtually, in some cases, starting *all over* again.

In this book, I will have some bold things to say to you. I am going to share about one of the most disturbing and heart-wrenching times of my life. I will be sharing about the circumstances that led to the closure of my involvement in and leadership of a ministry I started and to which I had dedicated my life. I will share about profound loss, and how, in that very loss, God created an exciting new path for my life and ministry. It's a modern-day story of Joseph whose dreams were dashed by rejection from his brothers, but in the end, he was used to save his brothers. Joseph said,

You intended to harm me, but God intended it for good to accomplish what is now being done, the saving of many lives (Gen. 50:20 NIV).

In my case, as you will soon see, God ended up leading me to start a new school that will over time train even more future leaders for Christ and His kingdom.

For those who are not familiar with my story, in 2014, the organization, United Liberia Inland Church Associates and Friends (ULICAF) that my wife and I co-founded and led for a decade was "hijacked." The mission and vision we had focused on for decades, in particular the creation and leadership of Liberia International Christian College (LICC), ended abruptly. A handful of divisive board members worked behind our backs and created an adversarial environment whereby other board members (some of them long-standing friends) turned against us and ultimately rejected our leadership. This nearly tore ULICAF and our friendships apart.

Maybe you have experienced rejection by those you considered close friends and ministry associates. Maybe you have given your life to some cause or organization only to see it ripped away before your eyes by those people who did not invest and sacrifice the time, energy, and money that you have.

If so, I want to encourage you by my story to be courageous and begin to take positive steps forward as you anticipate what God has for you next. At the time, you may feel isolated and alone. You may feel surrounded and attacked by forces you do not understand. Friends you have known for decades may draw away and begin to question your motives and be uncertain about what the true facts of the situation are.

My story is one that will show you how the believer is never alone. God can and will give you a new vision or dream for your life when a prior vision or ministry seems to just die. God can bring reconciliation and healing with those that you believed had betrayed you. This happened to me. Most importantly, God will guide you by His very presence and His power—comforting, leading, and teaching you new things about yourself and His faithfulness. You are not alone!

So, I offer you the *challenge and courage* to move on. In this story, you will find a clear and practical synthesis of the most important truths that Scripture and my life experience can teach us about starting over with courage and hope when you become blind-sided by a totally unexpected person or group. I am boldly offering my story as a victorious *key to winning* for every leader. Many leaders will attest to the fact that through great struggles, disappointments, and suffering we work out God's call on our life, as we daily submit to God's kingdom and his rule over our lives to enter to enter the kingdom of God. (see Acts 14:22 NIV)

The courage to move on is not out of your reach or my reach. When things appear to have gone terribly wrong, that is the time to make a commitment to move forward and not give up. In 2014, we experienced the death of our vision and leadership of ULICAF. I did not know that God had brand-new plans for me. I will bring you up to date (2023) with what I believe are the most amazing answers to prayer—answers which I consider miracles in my life.

You will be encouraged to see how God led me to start a new school. If God can do this in my life, when it seemed I had lost everything I worked for, then be encouraged. You will discover that you too can ignore your fears, silence your doubts, and start over with an even more powerful vision for your life.

My prayer is that you discover your God-sized dream or vision in the pages of this book, and you gain the courage to chase it. But your greatest legacy will not be your vision or dream; it will be the dreams you inspire in a new generation of leaders. You are not just a dreamer or a visionary; you are a dream-maker. **The God who is able to do immeasurably more than all you ask (or think) will accomplish something way beyond what you can imagine** (Sei's paraphrase of Ephesians 3:20).

Part 1

God's Plan for My Transition

Chapter 1: Our Original Plan for the Transition (The Genesis of Our Vision)

In 2000, we started United Liberia Inland Church Associates and Friends (ULICAF) as an outreach to Liberian immigrants in the United States and their American friends. Operating as an umbrella organization to United Liberia Inland Church across America, it grew very rapidly, expanding beyond what we would have thought possible. From 2000 to 2012, ULICAF's membership grew into thousands of members in states and cities all across the U.S.: Indiana, Minnesota, Georgia and the cities of Philadelphia, Chicago, Atlanta, and Pensacola, Florida.

For over 15 years we held annual conferences and taught the Word of God, encouraged our members to live wisely and fruitfully in America, and invited U.S. American pastors to join with us, a group of refugees from war-torn Liberia. Each conference brought a great sense of unity, and there was great fellowship amongst participants, mainly Liberian refugees. Liberians grew in self-confidence, firm in their faith and loving God. At each conference, Liberians and U.S. American Christians gave generously. Enough funds were raised to support several projects in Liberia. In 2003, this unity and generosity resulted in the plan to develop Liberia International Christian College (LICC). True to our vision, it was built and dedicated, and its door opened for operation in 2010.

The ULICAF ministry in Liberia extended beyond the college. Prior to opening the college, we funded the building of a United Liberian Inland Church (ULIC) leadership headquarters and a five-bedroom guest house in Monrovia. We received funds to build several local churches at various places in Liberia.

With the college built and running, the time had come for me to return to Liberia and continue the work of LICC. For the continued growth of the college, it was necessary to step aside from the day-to-day operations of ULICAF and focus on LICC. The original plan was for me to be a missionary-in-residence at LICC. The primary reasons for my return to Liberia included helping to recruit a new President, developing well-functioning and effective systems, establishing the various departments, and recruiting international instructional staff.

ULICAF would then continue to provide support. We had discussed this transition, but there were many details to work out. We planned for another leader to replace me as the leader of ULICAF in the United States.

In July 2014, we scheduled a conference in Minnesota to culminate the leadership transition. Invitations were extended to several church leaders in Liberia to join the occasion. Similarly, invitations were sent to hundreds of Liberian and American friends to join us. When the day came, we assembled just like at other conferences. With great celebration, my wife and I were commissioned to serve as missionaries in Liberia. A new Executive Director was commissioned to take charge of the American side leadership of ULICAF. Our transition plan was in full swing. At the conference, my second book *Vision, Valleys, & Victories* was launched, with copies distributed to all participants and mailed to our partners all across the United States.

Barely two weeks after the conference, my phone rang. The caller was Dr. Paul Miantona, the ULICAF Board Chair. He told me the Board had set up an emergency teleconference, and that I was needed. I then dropped everything that might interfere with this emergency call so that I would be available immediately for the call. "What was the important message of that call?" I wondered.

The Board planned to modify our agreed-upon salary arrangement. I was told that the board now considered its primary obligation was to take care of the financial needs of its new executive director. Then, to accommodate that plan, my salary would be reduced 50%! Only half of the salary would come from ULICAF. The other half would be paid by LICC, but *only* upon the approval by the *Liberian* Board. I asked for time to reflect on this new arrangement. Although it would make the job harder, if necessary, I could raise part of my support.

Later, the Board Chair delivered the message that some members of the Board took exception to even this arrangement and wanted it to be known that this was not a decision representing the whole board, but instead only of a few members. It became clear to me that this was more than a funding issue. I knew that I needed to find out exactly what was going on.

The situation kept getting worse. The next day, a new message was sent to me. This time, the board was not prepared to send a missionary at all, not even at half salary. Instead, I would be considered a *local* worker in Liberia. From that time on I was to be paid like any other local worker in Liberia, and *not* as a missionary.

"Why was being a missionary a problem for them?" I wondered. I was by that time a United States citizen. Serving as a local worker would require me or my employer to apply for a work permit from the government in Liberia. If the application was filed by my employer, it would require the employer to show the financial strength of the organization and the level of expertise needed to justify hiring someone like me with an American citizenship instead of a local Liberian.

Even though I was born and grew up as a Liberian, I would at that time be treated as an American applying for a Liberian job! Furthermore, if my application was approved, I would be required to pay taxes to the Liberian government. As a local worker with an American citizenship,

I would not be able to get Liberian social security benefits when I retired and would get reduced social security from the United States since I would not be paying anything into U.S. social security (for all intents and purposes, they would see I earned nothing) while I worked in Liberia.

This new arrangement was very confusing to me. This wavering by the Board with no explanation and my being left out of the discussion just made no sense. Up to this time I had never heard any personal accusations about me. I only heard about ULICAF's concern and final decision to focus on the salary of its new Director. I felt like something I had spent years leading and building seemed to be falling apart the very moment I stepped aside as Executive Director. Although we had planned for succession, I felt the Board was rushing to push me completely out of the picture. I felt that God was slamming a door closed—and I needed to get out.

Things began to become clearer to me when I heard that a few of the ULICAF leaders were having a teleconference from which I was excluded. I eventually interviewed some of the leaders, including Dr. Miantona, the Board Chair. For some, apparently, the conflict was driven by jealousy. Our seemingly easy success of founding and effectively leading ULICAF was envied. If they felt so, they did not understand all the work done behind the scenes in starting LICC. Perhaps they believed they could have easily done the same now that the school was complete and running! It was like they were trying to make the effort of those who contributed to the school a curse instead of a blessing. This is not God's way, of course. He gives His children good gifts. Unfortunately, we had entered a season similar to the biblical time of the judges when there was no king and everyone "did what was right in their own eyes" (Judges 17:6 NKJV). I did not think this would be good for either ULICAF or LICC and it both saddened and angered me.

A person may think their own ways are right, but the LORD weighs the heart (Prov. 21:2 NIV).

In his brilliant book *Chase the Lion*, Mark Batterson discusses a plot structure called "inciting incident" (Batterson, p. 22). It is a turning point, a tipping point, a point of no return. Inciting incidents come in two basic varieties: things that happen to you that you cannot control and things you make happen that you can control. Of course, even if something is out of your control, you can still control your attitude and reaction. You might not be responsible, but you are response-able. And it's the ability to choose your response that will likely determine your destiny. Some inciting incidents are perceived as positive, like a college scholarship or a job promotion. But one should never be too quick to judge an event as an apparent a blessing or a curse. What we perceive initially as positive sometimes turns out to have negative side effects, and what we perceive as negative often turns out to be the best thing that ever happened to us.

After an unsuccessful attempt at mending our differences in ULICAF, I felt like a complete failure. But if those attempts had succeeded, we never would have made the move to Liberia to found a new school. So in hindsight, that failure was one of the greatest opportunities that has been placed before me.

I haven't won the war with pride—it's a daily battle. But failure is one key to winning that war. It shows us what we are capable of, and in my case, it was not much! Without God's help, I am below average. That failed relationship/leadership taught me an invaluable lesson: "Unless the Lord builds the house, we labor in vain" (Psa. 127:1 NIV). The flip side is also true: What God opens, no one shuts, and what God shuts, no one opens (Rev. 3:7 NIV). The Apostle Paul puts it this way, "I can do all things through Christ who strengthens me" (Phil. 4:13 NIV).

One of the churches that was instrumental in helping us establish our original vision for ULICAF was Grace Church in Noblesville, Indiana. We have remained in contact. On November 16, 2022, David Rodriguez, Founding Pastor of Grace Church in Noblesville, Indiana, emailed me his blog with these observations about why we give up on each other. David explained that the observations were based on his experience from many decades of working with people, along with reading the research of social scientists and media. Taken all together, it has caused him to believe that American social networks have been in comprehensive and steady decline for decades.

Why do humans give up on each other? Here are his observations:

1. *Time pressures.* We have deleted connections from our packed lives. At the end of our frequently busy days and weeks, we opt for quiet moments on the couch. This is true of Americans as well as Liberian refugees who were working two to three jobs (16 to 20 hours a day sometimes) to make ends meet.

2. *Individualism.* America is not a collective culture which values interconnectedness between people; rather, we live in a culture that values assertiveness and autonomy.

3. *The Internet/technology.* Part of our inability to connect is due to screens and technology. Unfortunately, it is getting worse.

4. *Safety and social trust.* Political and cultural warfare have destroyed connections. Some former friends, family members and acquaintances are now enemies. They now seem unsafe to each other. Not knowing which tribe people

belong to has made even casual connections potentially dangerous.

5. *Me first.* Related to the individualism factor is a natural (but awful) self-absorption in ourselves that constantly runs all commitments through 'what's in it for me?' first.

6. *Tribalism.* In the Liberian setting, tribal discrimination is very visible. In our setting, ULICAF was mainly comprised of the Mano and Gio tribal groups from Nimba County, Northeastern Liberia. These two tribes are the majority inhabitants of Nimba County. These tribes constantly fight between themselves, primarily over power, and sometimes over land.

These factors are the devastating reality that, when you stop and think about it, makes our giving up on each other plausible.

For the last six years we have been developing a college preparatory high school in Liberia. Through the high school, the discipleship training, and entrepreneurship ministry, we have had the privilege of touching hundreds and thousands of lives. We anticipated that the best is yet to come. It is hard to imagine what our lives would be like if we hadn't taken that step of faith and been courageous to move on with this new vision. We would have forfeited so many blessings. But like every dream journey, it traces back to an inciting incident—a 5,000-mile trip from Fortville, Indiana to Liberia. We had no guaranteed salary when we packed our belongings into suitcases, but we knew God was calling us. To discover God's will, the Bible says you must "offer" your life to God—dedicate your treasures, time, relationships, and future to God's purposes. (see Romans 12:1)

What do you need to do to make your vision happen? Maybe it's taking that first step of faith or burning some bridges and cutting out some toxic relationships. After all, you cannot be double-minded. Maybe it's taking responsibility for something that has handicapped you for far too long and you now need to deal directly with it.

The Apostle Paul says his life is worth nothing to him unless he uses it for finishing the work God has assigned to him (Acts 20:24 NIV). Have you dedicated your life to God in faith in order to pursue your God-given vision? Yah and I had to ask ourselves this question and rededicate our lives to God. When Yah and I decided to move to Liberia, we did not have money, or salary, but we didn't let that stop us. We were aware of the problems, but we didn't wait to solve all the problems before starting out.

Chapter 2: A Story of Abandonment

As I write this, I now have the advantage of several years of deep reflection to analyze what really happened. When I first heard from the Board about their decision, I was very confused. I felt abandoned and angry. It seemed like each new call resulted in further loss of support from ULICAF. I could not help but think of the story of Jesus' own abandonment by his disciples in the Gospel of John.

The disciples responded to his teaching:

"This is a hard teaching. Who can accept it?"

Aware that his disciples were grumbling about this, Jesus said to them, "Does this offend you? Then what if you see the Son of Man ascend to where he was before! The Spirit gives life; the flesh counts for nothing. The words I have spoken to you—they are full of the Spirit and life. Yet there are some of you who do not believe."

For Jesus had known from the beginning which of them did not believe and who would betray him.

He went on to say, "This is why I told you that no one can come to me unless the Father has enabled them."

From this time many of his disciples turned back and no longer followed him.

"You do not want to leave too, do you?" Jesus asked the Twelve.

Simon Peter answered him, "Lord, to whom we shall go? You have the words of eternal life. We have come to believe and to know that you are the Holy One of God."

Then Jesus replied, "Have I not chosen you, the Twelve? Yet one of you is a devil!" (John 6:60–70, NIV)

These verses constitute the reaction of Jesus' disciples to His teaching on the "Bread of Life." Their real question is, "Who is able to hear it with appreciation?"

They found his teaching puzzling. How can one eat Jesus' flesh and drink his blood?

The response of many of the disciples was that of unbelief and rejection of him. John listed two groups and their reactions:

(1) The unchosen disciples' reaction of unbelief (vv. 60–66) and

(2) The chosen disciples' reaction of belief (vv. 67–71). After this teaching only a small nucleus of disciples remained (v. 67).

We are reminded that Jesus is all-knowing (omniscient). Jesus knew the heart of men, including his followers. He knew that many did not believe in Him as the Messiah and Son of God, so he did not entrust himself to them at this time. These unchosen disciples were simply attracted to the material blessings (food) and failed to understand the true significance of Jesus' teaching (v. 61).

In the face of unbelief, Jesus reiterated God's sovereign involvement in drawing people to him (v. 65). Jesus basically said to them, "Since you are offended by my claim to be the bread of life which came down from heaven, and my statement that you must eat my flesh, what would happen if you were to see the Son of Man going back to his original state? Would you be able to appreciate that higher glory at all?"

The claim that somehow, he offers himself as the bread of life can't be even compared to the greater supernatural claim that He came from eternity. He went on to remind them that his words had a heavenly origin and must be understood in a heavenly context. If they thought of eating his flesh and drinking his blood only in earthly terms, they were missing the point. It was not about eating his actual flesh and blood, but receiving his words which were life (v. 63).

Judas and some of the unchosen disciples who did not believe, were with Jesus physically, but their hearts were far from him. Many of his disciples turned back permanently and no longer followed him (v. 66).

Only God could change their indifferent hearts and draw them to surrender their lives to Him.

Now, we don't see Jesus chasing after them. No, He does something entirely different. Jesus turns to his disciples, the twelve, and said, "So what about you?"

Jesus never appeared desperate, manipulative, or controlling. He stayed mission-focused and others-centered. Jesus at times walked away from a toxic person, like Herod. Instead of arguing with Herod and trying to justify himself, Jesus remained silent (Luke 23:9 NIV). At the Last Supper Jesus knew that Judas was going to betray Him. He even spoke about it in advance. And yet, he allowed Judas to walk out of the room. He didn't chase after him. He didn't waste time trying to change Judas' mind. Instead, He spent his last minutes investing in His faithful, reliable disciples, praying right up until the moment He was arrested.

Jesus didn't need to defend himself. When Jesus was accused by the chief priests and the elders.

> He gave no answer. Then Pilate asked Him, 'Don't you hear the testimony they are bringing against you?' Jesus

made no reply, not even to a single charge—to the great amazement of the governor (Matthew 27:12–14 NIV).

When Jesus met the rich young ruler (see Matthew 19:21–23), Jesus discerned the motivation of the man's heart (his life's little god—the love of money). Yes, his reaction showed his attachment to wealth. When the young man could not let the money go, he determined to walk away from Jesus. Jesus never moved a step to run after him. He didn't make a second offer such as, "Please give only fifty percent instead of one hundred percent away." Jesus didn't beg the young ruler with appeals like, "Please come back; I need people to follow me."

No, Jesus turned to those who stayed with him (the reliable disciples) and taught them why it was difficult for a rich man to follow him and be an effective team player.

This is a lesson from Jesus: **Focus your discipleship on those that are faithful and reliable and are open to hearing the truth rather than chasing after the closed-minded person. In simple words, let those who are going go, and let those who are staying stay.**

Another example of the type of person we as leaders should find as our disciples is how Jesus dealt with Peter. Peter, often the spokesman for the disciples, on one occasion gave three reasons why they were determined to *stay* with Jesus:

1.   No one compares with Jesus (John 6:68 NIV).

2.   Jesus has the words of eternal life (John 6:68b NIV). Other teachers could repeat memorized prayers or sayings of their mentors, but their words had no power to change lives. On the other hand, Jesus's words were unique—they gave eternal life and could bring a person into a life of fellowship with God.

3. Jesus is the Holy One of God (John 6:69 NIV). Peter and the other eleven disciples concluded that Jesus is *the* "holy" one of God.

So how does this relate to what I went through? And to what you may be going through? Why the emphasis on this teaching? We are not Jesus, but we are his servants. What He has experienced, we may, too. In Matthew, Jesus said, "The student is not above the teacher, nor a servant above his master" (Matt. 10:24 NIV). When we attempt to do God's work even our closest allies at the time, our dearest team members, can lose confidence in their leader. They can be deceived by listening to the murmuring and doubts of others and fall away or turn against their leader (John 6:70–71 NIV).

I'm not saying every time someone disagrees with our decisions or direction in ministry, they are wrong. We can learn from constructive criticism. But there are those times when your former supporters lose their way and no longer walk with you.

As I moved forward with my mission for Liberia, I also found supporters who stood with me even as some close friends fell away. I would like to think that those who stuck with me were chosen by God to do so.

If you find yourself in similar circumstance, I recommend looking up first to God, but then look around and see those that still believe in you and your vision. Better to have one friend that stays with you then 20 undecided and ambivalent people in your ministry.

Chapter 3: Protecting the Dream

I'm sure many of you are familiar with the biblical account of the display of Solomon's wisdom and discernment in a judgment he made in the story of two women who each claimed a certain newborn baby was their own (see I Kings 3:16–27 NKJV).

In Israel, the King was the ultimate "judge" of the land. Every citizen could petition directly to him for a verdict. A case involving two prostitutes was most likely tried in the lower courts and then referred to King Solomon because they could not reach a decision.

The King allowed each woman to present her argument. Each woman claimed that she gave birth to a healthy boy in the same week that the other gave birth to a baby boy and that they lived in the same room. When one of the babies was found dead, neither woman would accept the dead child as her own. Both claimed the *living* child was hers.

The King, seeing the passionate disagreement, ordered his servants to cut the baby into two equal parts and give one half to each woman. This would conform to the law in Exodus 21:35 (although that law is about an animal not a child). The King knew that the woman that was lying would not object, but out of maternal compassion, the *real* mother would. As expected, the true mother could not bear the thought of her son being killed and was willing to give up her baby—even to the one who was not the real mother. The King then knew who the real mother was. (see I Kings 3:26–27 NKJV)

Now, to use that story as an illustration of my own experience: immediately after Yah and I were commissioned as missionaries to Liberia, three members of our board called a secret meeting. What they discussed planted a "seed of disunity" in the ULICAF Board. Who was speaking the truth? Who would be the ultimate judge like Solomon to discern the truth? How was I to defend myself? Who would rise up and render a wise decision about this division in the board?

Many Liberians that were the senior members of the board urged me to fight and hoped that the truth would prevail. Whatever I decided to do, my primary goal was to protect Liberia International Christian College (LICC) and the dream of this future school in which so many others had invested time, energy, and money. I thought that I could preserve both my relationship with ULICAF (America) and ULIC (Liberia).

LICC was my God-given vision. My family had invested itself in making LICC a reality. Yah and I had travelled across the United States meeting with donors in several cities, securing desks and chairs, computers, and books for the library. In order to save money, we refused to spend money on hotels; instead, we spent nights in the homes of Liberians or anyone who would host us.

For example, in 2002, prior to LICC's opening, I sent out a series of emails in the U.S. and Europe to obtain furniture for the school. An unknown lady from Amsterdam, Holland responded. She wrote, "A high school in my city is closing down, and they are willing to give away their desks and chairs, but you have to pay for shipping them to Liberia." At first, I thought it was a scam. However, when I verified this request, I found out that this lady was a follower of Christ, and she and her husband taught at the University of Liberia in the late 1970's. ULICAF covered the shipping, and 350 pieces of furniture (desks, chairs and tables) were sent to Liberia.

In 2016, my older son Deizie and I drove 30 hours round trip from Indianapolis to Pennsylvania to gather 65 flat-screen computers donated by a Social Security office. In other words, there is not a single item of the furniture, books, or computers that we did not receive through networking with others that God brought to us.

Throughout those years of collecting supplies and fundraising, my whole family invested our time and energy into creating this wonderful connection of Liberian and American friends in ULICAF. Legally, only one member signed with me on the original document to obtain a non-profit status for ULICAF.

I realize that at the time when I lost the trust of some of my closest associates, the one Greater than Solomon would be my final judge on my life's calling and work. I knew that, ultimately, I had to continue my ministry in Liberia even if it was not with ULICAF. It was like the Lord was speaking to me:

> "This is your life's work to which I have called you and your wife; therefore, you must do it. Go preach the Gospel yourself and train others to do so, too. That is your life's object and aim."

We had started what many consider to be the first college founded by indigenous people in Liberia, West Africa This was an accomplishment, though initiated by me, and it could not have been a reality without the partnership of many Liberians (in America and Liberia) along with our American friends.

Because I was unwilling to take a course that I felt might threaten the college's future, I walked away from ULICAF so that it might continue under the leadership of others. If I really cared about the ministry (just like the real mother that really cared about her baby), I would be willing to give up the "baby of this ministry" so that young people in Liberia could have an opportunity for a college education.

If I had gone the legal route and tried to get a judgment in court, the court could have issued an injunction which would shut down all activities of the institutions or organization for months or even years!

For example, as I wrote this chapter, the election of officers of the Press Union of Liberia (PUL is an umbrella organization of journalists in Liberia) was currently in a civil court in Monrovia. All activities of the organization are on hold, including its leadership election until the investigation is completed.

Here is another example of the dangers of pursuing legal action. In Nimba County, the senators and representatives (referred to as Nimba Caucus) elected from the county every year has a "sitting" (a meeting) to discuss the budget for the next year and decide on which projects should be funded. Unfortunately, in July 2020 there was an issue with the voting process. They debated the use of a ballot box or *counting heads*. Due to this disagreement, the sitting ended up in court where the judge issued an injunction until the issue could be settled. There will now be no progress on the projects. The 21 yellow machines (construction equipment) were not moving because of the disagreement.

LICC will need continued support for many years. It was important to have a viable organization in America to allow Liberians and our American friends to continue providing aid to LICC. I was unwilling to take any steps that I felt might endanger its success. It never was "mine," in a sense of ownership, and I would be a foolish steward to take steps in anger that might endanger its future.

In this matter, God granted me wisdom. I believe everyone's life has moments of decision that dictate the course of that person's life. If we fail to take action, we forfeit the future He has planned for us.

On April 4, 2016, I drafted my resignation letter. Despite the request of many board members to fight the others' decisions, I stepped aside so that LICC could continue with its purpose of educating Liberians. A copy of my letter of resignation is included on the next page.

April 4th, 2016

Mr. Dehpue Zuo
Acting President, Liberia International Christian College
Board of Trustees
Ganta City, Nimba County

Dear Mr. Zuo,

I am writing this letter to submit my resignation as the President of Liberia International Christian College. I plan to officially step down on Monday July 4th, at 12:00 pm, a day after LICC's 2015−16 graduation.

Thanks to the board and all ULICAF members who gave me the opportunity to serve our great institution. I am proud of what we all have achieved since the establishment of LICC.

I have particularly helped the college raised the needed funding to purchase the 24.5 acres of land, developed the current infrastructure, and hired about 50 competent faculty and staff, and held a clear course toward a bright future.

I care deeply about our institution, and the continuing "lack of agreement, almost every pertinent issue relating to effective operation and growth" have become too great of a distraction to our mission of educating students. It was a very difficult decision, but I believe it is the right course of action for LICC at this time.

Blessings to you and all your great leaders,

SEI

Chapter 4: The Courage to Move On

Courage is needed when we face the unknown in a number of different circumstances. We need courage when we experience failure in any task or job. We must move on, trusting that God has something better for us. We need courage when we deal with the fear; we have to obediently follow a proper direction in life even though we might be misunderstood for our decisions.

One of my greatest lessons in courage came as a child, although I didn't even think to call it courage at the time:

As far back as I can remember as a child, on the 24th of August, Liberians have celebrated the birth of our flag. Liberian history reveals that Matilda Newport, a free slave descendant, made the flag. The flag is modeled after the flag of the United States. Its colors are red, blue, and white, and represent our nation's sovereignty. It's visibly displayed and flown outside on all important government buildings as well as on all academic institutions across the nation, including Riverview Village School where I went to elementary school.

When I was growing up, all grade schools around the country paid homage to the flag by performing indoor and outdoor programs in the city or village centers. Primarily, the outdoor program included various forms of marching drills in front of a large audience comprised of parents, grandparents, and civil and political leaders. Judges were selected to reward the school with the best performance. At our local competition, year after year, our school in Riverview Village, tried very hard, but never won once. That was until one special year in which Riverview Village School finally won first place and was rewarded with a golden trophy! Our village was joyous.

Later we heard the story behind this accomplishment. Our Master Drill Sergeant had been under terrible pressure from the village. Every year our parents felt sick to their stomachs for their children's failure to get an award. Some parents wanted to remove the drill sergeant while others requested that he be given one more chance.

The Master Drill Sergeant knew that he would be replaced if our performance didn't improve. Although it was an honorary position, it still came with community respect. The drill sergeant wanted us to do well for our town's pride, and he also wanted to keep his position! He knew that the training we had been receiving wasn't working. He could have resigned, but he decided to try one more time.

Some time prior to the next celebration, he quietly departed the village and visited the other drill sergeants to learn their methods of winning competitions. When he returned, he thought to himself, "I now have the solution." He focused on two simple drill commands: "forward move" and "about face." That was it! They were the only winning commands our school needed. I am not joking. It had really worked for other schools as well.

So, when the Master Drill Sergeant reappeared, our school was placed on lockdown. We engaged in a crash course of similar practices, built around the technique, "Forward Move" and "About Face." When the drill sergeant gave the "Forward Move" command, we marched with rapid, fearless speed. To onlookers, it appeared that we would crash headfirst right into the wall. But just before we would have crashed into the wall, the second command came with his thundering voice, "About Face," and in the twinkling of an eye, we would flip backward or turn around and march just as rapidly in the opposite direction.

At our local competition that year, the judges called for us to repeat the exercise several times because some thought we would fail to make a successful maneuver the second time. Perhaps they were thinking we would become fearful and not wait for the Master Drill Sergeant's last second command and turn around on our own before any command was given. We never did make that error! In the end, we received the winner's reward—a trophy!

Even though I wouldn't have used the word *courage* back then to describe it, now I think the Master Drill Sergeant showed courage to not resign, and to think of ways to improve our performance. He took decisive action. We, his students, showed courage by marching forward rapidly and trusting that our Drill Sergeant would give us a perfectly-timed command right before we would have plowed into the wall!

The term "courage or courageous" entered my mental dictionary in the 1980s. During my early years of developing a strong faith in God, I joined a youth group. The group engaged in intense weekly Bible study and Scripture memory. One of the Scriptures we memorized was God's encouragement through Moses to Joshua:

> **"I not commanded you? Be strong and courageous. Do not be afraid; do not be discouraged for the Lord your God will be with you wherever you go" (Joshua 1:9 NIV).**

Moses had seen the burning bush where God's presence was made real to him. For forty years God had used Moses as an untiring mediator between God and His people. It is extremely difficult to succeed such a leader. He had fearlessly faced Pharaoh and his threats. We all know the story, that he eventually, with God's empowerment, led God's people out of Egypt.

When Moses died, God called Joshua to take over. Joshua's new responsibility was to lead a whole community, a new generation of millions of Israelites into an unfamiliar land and conquer it. Joshua faced enormous challenges. There were giants in the land. There were definitely going to be physical battles with the enemy. They didn't have homes of their own. Without God it would be frightening—even impossible. Joshua proved to be an outstanding leader.

All leaders will face the unknown. They will question their own abilities to accomplish the tasks before them.

What is the land you need to take over? What are the giants (obstacles) in the territory you are trying to conquer (a challenging job responsibility, a new move to an unfamiliar area, a difficult relationship, a temptation to resist, etc.)?

Successful leadership requires bold decision-making followed by daring action. It doesn't mean that fear will be non-existent. *Courage is acting in the very presence of fear.* The fear of failure is a natural phenomenon and a powerful emotion. We all have experienced normal fear at one time or another. However, what matters most is what you do with fear.

What was my Joshua moment? I was about to resign from an organization I had spent many years building and leading. What would I do next? How would I provide for my family? Along with an attitude of courage, I also needed to act and initiate some new direction for my life. How would I generate momentum to move forward in my life?

In different times and in different ways, Christ Jesus offers us a simple proposition: Follow me beyond what you can control. Follow me beyond where your own strength and competencies can take you. Follow me beyond what is affirmed or risked by the crowd—and you will experience my very presence, my power, my wisdom and my love!

Bringing a Dream Team Together

Second Samuel 23 lists 37 names of David's best friends, his closest confidants. Not only was their courage unmatched, but their loyalty to

David was undivided. After reading this story, I asked myself, "What drew these men to David? What turned these rebel men into a band of brothers? What would entice them to cast lots with a foreigner? God, what are you teaching me from this story?" Undoubtedly, these men saw something extraordinary in David. They saw David had a God-sized dream. And the Lord said to me, "this is what will draw people to you—a God-sized vision." Choose your friends carefully and prayerfully. The people you are closest to will help you figure out your God-given vision or they will hinder you. So, it is important to surround yourself with people who are pursuing God's will and vision.

Christian Leadership Training International (CLTI), as an organization, began when I invited a few friends to brainstorm a new vision. Of course, I prayed about a new course of action. I knew that if I got stuck in bitterness or focused too much on what I "lost," I couldn't move forward. I could have become paralyzed with fear or resentment. Someone once said, "Too much analysis leads to paralysis."

As I thought back on the early years of United Liberia Inland Church Associates and Friends (ULICAF), we had always needed God's daily intervention to accomplish the dream school that eventually became Liberia International Christian College (LICC). What was my next step?

First, I stopped having repeated conversations about my loss of the ministry I had developed for years. Second, I decided to "give myself some grace." We tend to extend grace to others and give them "second" chances, but we are too tough on ourselves. Why couldn't the next 5 years of my life far outshine the last 5 years? We have heard "rags to riches" stories of people that bounced back financially, or amazing comebacks in sports, or failure in relationships that are later replaced by even better and more lasting friendships. Health lost can be regained through proper nutrition and exercise and God's healing power.

I learned to stop pursuing perfection and instead began pursuing the best version of me *in this season*, based on what I know right now. I often tell people I might not be the smartest person in the world, but I am one of the most resilient—or at least I am working on this. I have discovered that reversals and disappointment are often the gateway around the corner for success!

Janet Jennings in *The Blue and the Grey*, includes a quotation from Napoleon Bonaparte about two kinds of courage—regular courage and two-o'clock in the morning courage. "He contends that the rarest attribute among military generals 'is two-o'clock in the morning courage.'" Getting my new vision off the ground and ready to move forward was a two-o'clock in the morning courage for me. This one act of courage totally changed my life. The same will be true of you. You are one decision away from a totally new life. It will be the toughest decision you ever make, the scariest risk you ever take, but it will be the most life-changing moment ever for your life.

Here is my earlier morning courage theory: Your favorite scripture will become the foundational text of your life. I take mine from Joshua 1:9 (quoted on p. 39). This scripture underscores who I want to be, what I want in life, and what I believe about God. Sometimes we get afraid or we get so busy climbing the success ladder that we miss God's vision and that leads to regret. We will regret that we left God-ordained opportunities on the table. We will regret not pursuing a God-size vision because we let rejection or fear dictate our pathway. The only way to tap into God's potential for our lives is to step forward, trusting and obeying God. God's dream for your life is so much bigger and better than you could ever imagine. (Eph. 3:20) If you focus on yourself, or your own weakness or temptation, or never making mistakes, you won't make a difference. You need a God-given vision that is bigger and better than what you are going through right now.

Part 2

New Dream, New Organization, New School

Chapter 5: My New Mission

Even after transitioning from LICC, my life was still dedicated to the education of the children of Liberia. But I had entered a new chapter of my life. I began to feel an answer building up within me. There was something I'd wanted to do for a long time. However, occupied with the ongoing responsibilities of LICC, it was a dream that I had to lay aside. Now, with a closed door, God had allowed me time to focus on that dream. I wondered if it was time to build a school to *prepare* students for college. What do you need to do to make your dream come true? Maybe it is taking the first step of faith. One thing that I am certain of is it will take courage!

With our transition from ULICAF and LICC complete, we scheduled a trip back to Liberia once again. This time, we went to explore further what God would have us do. In the first week or two, several visitors came by to see Yah and me. One visitor after another expressed their deep regrets about the situation in which we seemingly had to start all over again. They encouraged us, though, because they believed that if we just trusted God, there would be a new ministry for us in Liberia.

One of the visitors was a young woman, Nohn. She was a former student at LICC and her words of encouragement that our purposes in Liberia were not finished yet had a special meaning and impact on us. Let me share why. Nohn confided in us that she could relate to and "identify" with us. We had been her mentor and coach and financial sponsor during her study at LICC. After the civil war and graduation from LICC she later became Mayor of Gompa. However, after a new administration under President Ellen Sirleaf Johnson began to lead the country, she was dismissed without any explanation from the new government leadership. She received no appreciation or compensation for her years of service.

When we first met again, she was angry and desperate. She had neither job nor money. According to Nohn, her dismissal as mayor was based on her lack of official education after her high school graduation. At that time, we presented her with a financial scholarship to pursue two years of college at LICC. It was like a gift of manna from heaven (See Exodus 16). She graduated with an Associates in Arts degree in accounting and finance from LICC.

It was quite amazing that after Nohn completed her studies she was hired by the government as a Liberian Revenue Collection Agent at the Guinea-Liberia border in Gompa. She was now in a position to offer us help when we most needed it. She specifically questioned us and wanted to know if we were just on a short visit and would soon return to America, or if God might be leading us to establish a brand-new school. We told her that that we were exploring and praying for a new direction from the Lord.

Then she said, "Well, I am glad you came back to Liberia. I heard that you had resigned from LICC and moved permanently back to America. However, if you ever need land to develop for the ministry, please let me help. My family has a huge piece of land. I will be glad to gather my brothers to go with you and show you the location, and if you like the area, I will ask my family to give you any amount for little or nothing."

Nohn was quite generous in her offer, but after checking the location, we decided to not build a school there. It was a great piece of property, but the location was outside of the perimeter of the city center of Gompa.

Although the land did not work out, we were quite thankful for the support Nohn gave us. We were excited because not only was Nohn someone that directly and practically benefitted from LICC, but most importantly, she gave us the timely comfort we needed during our transition to the next chapter in our ministry.

There is a lesson here for all leaders. *Even leaders need encouragement from those we have helped in the past.* Out of the ten lepers that Jesus healed (see Luke 17:12-18), only *one* returned to say thank you to Jesus! In our case, more than one person has returned to say thank you for our work at Liberia International Christian College (LICC). Presently, four out of our first LICC graduates are serving in full-time staff positions with Christian Leadership Training International (CLTI), our new organization. Many others are helping us by volunteering in other areas such as networking on behalf of CLTI.

After leaving LICC, God gave us the courage to move forward and to make plans to advance His kingdom according to Jesus' own words: "Go and make disciples of all nations . . . . I am with you till the end of the age" (Matthew 28:19–20 NIV). In our situation, it was beginning to look like that would be to one day build a school for young students (elementary to high school) and disciple them to be future leaders in Liberia.

Marie was the next one to visit me. Several years before, we had purchased an acre of land from Marie to build our present home in Liberia. During our conversation with her she indicated that one of the young ladies that had helped with our laundry in the past had now moved to the city. Her father was a chief in a nearby village that was selling land. The village now was within Gompa city limits. It just happened that recently the village was being pressured to sell the large tract of tribal land it had owned for decades. They had passed it on from one generation to the next without developing any building on it. Marie called the chief and arranged for us to meet with him. The chief was happy to see us and invited all his elders and youths to show us the land.

47

The land was five acres, not the ten or twenty acres we had imagined. Immediately, we sensed we could compromise on quantity to shoot for this very strategic location. We just knew that this was the perfect property for a new school! It was less than two miles from the city center and a main highway nearby was pending construction in the near future. After divine intervention, from the initial price of $50,000, we settled on $20,000 for the five acres of land.

One of the defining moments in our dream journey as Christian Leadership Training International (CLTI) was the decision for Yah and me to first give toward the purchase of the five acres of land before anyone else could give. It was a financial statement of faith based on a core conviction: God will bless us in proportion to how we give to His kingdom work.

That night as we reflected in bed about this amazing property we praised God for an answer to prayer—"where two or three gather in Jesus" name, you shall have what you ask." That night, my wife and I knelt before Jesus. During our prayer, Yah asked that we follow the Old Testament principle of "First Give, then Ask" (see II Chronicles 29). There was only $2,000 in our savings accounts. My wife suggested that we give it all. The next morning, we called our daughter, Olivia, to write the check for that amount and mail it to CLTI's Treasurer. Now, we were free to ask our partners for help, and we did just that.

Next, we sent out letters and emails to several friends in the States and asked for their financial support. About two weeks after the mails, we received several generous donations. Then we had a total of $17,000 that we used to make our initial payment.

Nothing sets us up for God's provision like a sacrificial giving. If you want God to bless you beyond your ability, try giving beyond your means. I am not speaking of just material rewards; it's not what we are after. What we are after is an eternal reward in heaven. Jesus' promise still holds true:

> "Give and it will be given to you. A good measure, pressed down, shaken together and running over, will be poured into your lap. For with the measure you use, it will be measured to you" (Luke 6:38 NIV).

We also asked the landowner for time to pay the property off and we set up a payment plan. The chief gave us three months to make a full payment, or we would lose three lots off the land. This gave us a sense of urgency.

We returned to the States. After two months had passed, although we had raised some money, we still had no indication that we would have the balance of the $3,000 we owed in time. Then, God brought a friend. Jay Skinner called me and said he had scheduled a business meeting near Lawrence, Indiana where I was staying. He asked me if I was free to get a cup of coffee. During our coffee time, he asked me about the project. I was bold and let him know about our outstanding debt. Immediately, he committed to write the full amount of the remaining balance and returned with a check for $3,000 the next day. I immediately transferred the funds to Liberia. We had raised the full $20,000 and we met our obligation and paid off the debt. God had moved in a few people and touched their hearts.

After the purchase was completed, we made a trip to Liberia, established ownership by surveying the land, and obtained title to the property. We then returned to the States and reported the good news to CLTI's Board of Directors.

We next had to decide the timing of breaking ground and laying the foundation. We wanted to start as soon as possible and began making all the necessary preparations. We scheduled and broke ground on May 19, 2018, less than two full years after my resignation from Liberia

International Christian College. We invited local leaders, people in business, religious leaders, and several Ganta community schools' leaders for the ground-breaking event. Many at that time made cash contributions or donated materials. More than 200 bags of cement were gathered that day!

CLTI's goal was to build a college preparatory high school. This would be the first faith-based college prep high school in the whole region. We planned to offer a rigorous course of study focused on preparing students for college and university admission. Our goal was to significantly improve the performance of Nimba County students. Historically, their test scores for the mandatory annual national examination were very low. Our plan was to create a premier institution to equip the future leaders and developers of Liberia by providing a strong foundation of practical knowledge and academic excellence to ensure the students' success in higher education.

In January 2018, we had contracted with Engineering Ministries International (EMI) to provide the design services. This was an organization we had worked with before when we developed LICC. EMI is a non-profit organization that provides design services for evangelical Christian ministries in developing countries that are both helping the poor and advancing the gospel of Christ. It is comprised of a network of engineers, architects, and surveyors who donate their services free or offer much discounted service fees.

For ten days starting on February 8, 2018, twelve members of the EMI team came to Gompa to work with us. The team provided the following services: site surveying, master plan, architectural and conceptual design, water supply and wastewater disposal plans, access road design, and electrical supply lines. Then, Peter Ewers Architecture, a Christian-owned firm in Golden, Colorado, finalized the drawing for the 16,900 square feet building. The building has the capacity to accommodate 1,200 to 1,500 students, and the cost estimate was projected at $350,000, excluding furniture.

On August 19, 2018, we commenced the construction of the college preparatory high school with the digging of the foundation. We continued to trust the Lord for funding, and gradually we continued the construction work as God provided.

How much is your vision worth? Is it worth $20,000? How about $100,000? What price are you willing to pay?

When God gives a vision, He makes provision. But in my experience, you often have to take a financial step of faith first. So, how much is your vision worth? Count the cost. Pay the price, and the rest will be an amazing story of God's provision!

Deciding to Act

Your vision is worthless until you act on it. God gave Moses the dream or vision of leading the children of Israel after four hundred years of slavery, but Moses had to make the decision to confront Pharaoh. During the decision period, you must act on two things. First, you must invest. You must decide to invest your time, your finances, your reputation and your energy in the things that will advance your pursuit of God's vision. You must stop all excuses and plunge head-on into it. Say, "God, I am in, and will not procrastinate any longer. I am ready to do whatever you tell me to do. I am ready to go wherever you want me to go." Second, let go of your insecurity. You cannot move forward in faith without trusting God for your life and your family's lives (see Proverbs 20:25). This is not about making a hasty decision. It is about making the right decision. Most often quick decisions are easy, but can also be wrong. But a spiritual decision requires prayer for God's guidance. So, spend time reading the Word of God until you discover the truth revealed, and then act on the truth. Ask yourself what God is teaching you through this particular truth or biblical principal.

Next, gather facts before making the final decision. As discussed in chapter five, both Yah and I are nationals of Liberia, but we made several fact-finding trips. Upon arrival, we talked to many people. We interviewed them and listened carefully as we sought advice from wise church leaders and community chiefs. We did not take any steps for granted.

We had decisions to make. You have decisions to make. You must discern what God is calling you to do, and the next steps you need to take. These are the decisions that will determine your destiny.

Digging the foundation

I am asked from time to time if my experience building LICC helped when it came time to build CLTI's school. As you would expect, the answer is absolutely "yes." However, this time not only did I have a better understanding of the construction process, but I had a large network of contacts and supporters! Many of those who helped us with LICC are now helping us build this new high school.

What is the one step you can take today to discover God's revealed truth so you can make wise decisions?

Celebrating the completion of their work

From Dream Team to Non-Profit

To support our planned ministry in Liberia, we began the process of setting up a non-profit in the U.S. For Christian Leadership Training International (CLTI) to be an official non-profit in the U.S., it needed approval from the U.S. government. We had processed United Liberia Inland Church Associates and Friends' non-profit legal status through a law firm in Indianapolis. Unfortunately, their cost was prohibitive for a start-up organization like CLTI.

Fortunately, over the years, I had searched for a professional service provider whose fees were less expensive. Because of our time with ULICAF, we developed a broad network of contacts. One of those contacts, Lori, was in Florida. Her fee to file the paperwork for a 501(c)3 (the standard U.S. non-profit designation) was only $499.00. I quickly charged the amount on my credit card, and she proceeded to work on our non-profit status. In less than a month, Lori forwarded the documents to me for my signature, and we proceeded to immediately mail them to the Internal Revenue Service (IRS).

To create a non-profit, both state and federal approval are needed. A document of this type usually takes a month for state approval, but three to six months for federal approval. As expected, in less than a month we received the state approval. We patiently waited and finally we got our approval from the Federal government and the assigned ID number, which now allowed our friends in the United States to make tax-deductible gifts to CLTI.

Yah and I were in Liberia when the Federal approval was emailed to me. With great excitement, I forwarded it to all our CLTI's Board of Directors. We were now official and off and running!

Our new organization is focused on three main areas: Discipleship, Entrepreneurship, and Education—which I will discuss in the next few chapters.

Chapter 6: Discipleship

My ministry has been touched and greatly influenced by the lives of many people. Some of the most powerful influences have been men and women of God who came alongside Yah and me at just the right time to encourage us and help us grow in our faith. Without the insight and help of these faithful Christians our ministry would not be as effective as it now is. What they modeled for me in their lives as followers of Jesus, I have tried to put into practice as I disciple young Liberian Christians.

The Genesis of Faith (The Story of Sammy Morris)

One night in the 1970s, I joined a few friends to watch a documentary about the life of a young native Liberian named Sammy Morris. As we left our village and walked under the moonlight, we were excited to hear the story of "Sammy" who was born into a Krue tribe in Southeastern Liberia. He had been kidnapped by a neighboring tribe and ended up being a slave to the tribal chief. Sammy's father was unable to buy his release. Kept as a hostage, he was subjected to constant whipping by his slave master. One day, after a really severe beating, and with the threat of execution hanging over him, he said he heard God speak to him telling him to immediately flee and run for his life.

Amazingly, he escaped the terror of his slave master and arrived at a coastal rubber plantation where he met an American missionary lady. The missionary took Sammy in and mentored and discipled him for almost a year. She even gave him the name Sammy Morris (which was the name of her sponsor back in America). One day, in a mentoring class focusing on the Holy Spirit, Sammy asked the missionary lady how he could teach his people to know more about the power of the Holy Spirit. The lady told Sammy that her teaching was not adequate to prepare him to evangelize his people, but she would pray that Sammy could go to a seminary in America.

Eventually, God answered both Sammy's and the missionary's prayer, and Sammy travelled to New York City in 1891. The long boat ride across the ocean was a challenge for Sammy who had never travelled outside his country. The work assigned to him in exchange for his passage was hard and dangerous and he was beaten a number of times. When he arrived in New York, God showed him favor. When he got off the boat, the first person he asked for help knew the minister he was looking for. With God's help on his journey, eventually he found his way to Taylor University in Indiana to learn about biblical faith and about the Holy Spirit.

After watching the documentary, I was impressed with Sammy's spiritual hunger and desire to teach his people about the Holy Spirit. During that time, I had no idea where in the world Indiana or Taylor University were located. Nor did I think I would ever visit Indiana!

Thirty-five years after that transforming night watching the Sammy Morris video, I met a young student from Taylor University at Grace Church in Noblesville, Indiana. On that occasion, Yah and I were standing in the hallway of Grace sharing with others our financial needs and wanting to raise funds to establish a college in Liberia. The goal of the college was to train pastors to evangelize my people in Liberia. When she heard that I was from Liberia, she asked if I knew anything about Sammy Morris. When I said "Yes," she told me she was a student at Taylor where Sammy had come for training with the goal of returning to Liberia to reach his people for Christ and tell them about the Holy Spirit. I felt speechless; this was quite a coincidence!

That same week, my friend Jon Lieberman and I arranged a visit to Taylor. When we first arrived, we saw a statue of Sammy Morris and a student hall named in honor of Sammy Morris. What touched me most on the visit was the vivid resemblance of this statue to myself. Sammy could have been my brother. When I looked at the picture of me standing next to the statue, I saw that we had the same color and style of hair, dark face, broad nose, and big protruding lips, as  well as being similar in height. Sammy's story is more than 125 years old. (To learn more about Sammy Morris and Taylor University, see www.taylor.edu/about/Samuel-morris and see notes on the statues in the References at the end of this book.)

Sammy only lived a year and a half before he suddenly became ill and died, but one of the impacts of his life was saving Taylor University from financial difficulties. The school was facing a time of economic depression in the late 1800s. Sammy's devotion to Jesus and a remarkable prayer life brought revival to the school. After his death many students wanted to be missionaries. A revival broke out at the university. His story was printed in a book which thousands of people bought. The funds from this book helped the university to get out of debt and buy the land where the school exists in Upland, Indiana. Year after year, Sammy's story has been used to raise millions of dollars to provide an academic community that continues to have an outstanding faculty and programs. It is a premier academic institution that not only excels nationally among small universities but promotes Christ and biblical values. Taylor has helped prepare students from all over the world to be led by the Holy Spirit to impact every area of culture and work as teachers, businesspeople, lawyers, doctors, etc., as well as those who go into fulltime Christian ministry. Sammy's testimony has impacted and given courage to many international students to return to their homeland to advance the Good News.

Sammy has often been called "Africa's missionary to America." Through his short time at Taylor University, he had an immediate and long-term impact on Taylor, the surrounding community, and eventually the world. Sammy had a passion for street evangelism, so he visited the local town's people and local churches. Unfortunately, he died before completing his training to return to Liberia to teach his people about the Holy Spirit directly. He contracted pneumonia during a cold Indiana winter and died rather quickly and went home to be with Jesus. He never married, never saw his earthly family after leaving for America, and did not see his 30th birthday. Yet, his impact for Jesus is eternal.

I want to die like Sammy! No, not from pneumonia. I want to die doing what I love to do, doing what God has called me to do. I want to pursue God-sized visions until the day He calls me into heaven. This is the way to go!

Sammy never got to complete his education. I have been blessed, though, to complete my graduate education in America (Th.M., Master of Theological Studies from Western Theological Seminary, 1996, and a Ph.D. in Educational Leadership and Policy Studies, 2001, from Loyola University) and return to Liberia to help my people. Today, CLTI Ministry is attracting young men and women who want to discover the truth about life, mature in Christ, and ultimately fulfill the great commission (Matt. 28:18–20). We are working to increase opportunities for emerging Christian leaders and work with them to learn God's Word and principles of leadership.

So, who is Jesus sending you to? For CLTI, *Disciple Making* is a key ministry focus in Liberia. In 2015, God called and launched our team and partners in the city of Gompa, the second largest and fastest growing commercial city. (The capital city Monrovia is the largest.) We focus on the students in the inner-city high schools and college students also. Initially, we selected 12 high school and college students to meet and study in our home every Sunday afternoon. From this first group, we identified and trained our future leaders.

Jefferson Polay is one of our co-leaders. Jefferson is a theology student at African Bible College University (about 60 miles north of Ganta) and is pursuing biblical studies to become a pastor and a church planter. His leadership influence and passion for making disciples has already made him a key player on our team.

Jefferson Polay

Resources We Use and Their Transformative Impact

The *Bible* is our primary textbook. However, we use a training manual: *Finding YOUR Place in the World,* written by Joe Williamson (available on Amazon). *Finding YOUR Place in the World* introduces the tSOAR (the Time, Truth, Trust, Surrender, Obey, Abide and Reconciliation) concepts and the process is appropriate to anyone—a seeker, a new believer, a growing believer or a mature believer. The book's

premise is that life's deepest question, "Why am I here?" can find its answer in God's Word. When we spend meaningful time with God's truth, we discover the ultimate peace and purpose of life which is "to know God personally, and to love and serve Him and enjoy Him forever." The Father shapes our character (who we are) and our calling (what we do) and grounds us in Christ, providing the stability to weather the storms of life. As we abide in Him, we continue to bear more fruit in our lives.

One of the locations we use for discipleship training is Pastor Lombaye's local church building in Gompa. Every Saturday afternoon from 5:30 to 6:30 p.m. we have meetings. We are so thankful for this pastor making this location available for us. Both he and his wife are regular attendees of the training too.

A couple of months before I wrote this chapter, my wife and I met Pastor Lombaye and his wife Elizabeth. Pastor Lombaye invited us to worship with their church congregation. After our initial visit, he came back and asked me if I would preach sometime and bring a message from God's Word. Yah and I had a very busy schedule and eventually we had the chance to visit again. We felt the Lord prompting us to talk about *disciple-making*.

We were impressed by Pastor Lombaye's and his wife's diligence and faithfulness. Finally, I had this sudden realization: Pastor Lombaye had graduated from an Assembly of God Bible College in Monrovia, but his wife, Elizabeth, was among the first graduates of LICC, the pastoral training college we had helped to start some years ago! Yah and I started worshipping at Pastor Lombaye's church.

Pastor and Mrs. Lombaye planted their current church in 2007 and it has grown to over 150 members. They have also helped to plant five other churches in the city. The church in the background of their photo was built by faith alone with donations from the congregation.

Jesus gave his initial instructions to those first disciples at a specific point in time in their ministry. The good news about the kingdom was to be proclaimed first to his Jewish people, Israel. After his death and resurrection, Jesus commanded the message to be taken to *all* nations (see Matthew 28:19). Jesus has called us to also to go and make disciples. Our heavenly Father's desire is to bring the message of reconciliation to all the people groups of the world. Yah and I cannot go to every nation. But we can help those struggling poorer young students all around us in Liberia. We are called to Liberia and our primary focus is high school and college students, the new generation of Christian leaders for Liberia.

Life-Transforming Principles Learned from Focus on Making Disciples

What life transforming principles are we learning as we focus on making disciples? Jesus still calls *ordinary* men and women to go and make disciples and do *extraordinary* things. Although the churches in Liberia have many "attendees," there are so many church goers that don't reflect His character in their daily lives.

In our study and training in our discipleship program, we sit at the feet of Jesus, the teacher, and listen to His words in the gospel. We then ask ourselves what the Word says, what it means, what it meant to the first hearers and recipients of God's Word, and what we are going to do based on what we just studied. This is real discipleship—putting God's Word into action—being doers and not hearers only of the Word.

Our distinct ministry focus:

Spiritual Parenting: We develop students in the context of *community*—daily interaction with their teachers and other students and accountability to those in leadership so they can humbly learn from their mistakes as well as gain courage from their victories.

Spiritual Generations: We are not content until those we help are also helping others to grow in maturity and reproduce spiritually.

Spiritual Transformation: We believe that man was intended to live by every word that proceeds from the mouth of God. Here, we focus on transformation because of interacting with the Scriptures.

Joe Williamson (shown with Sei) is the founder of tSOAR, a discipleship ministry. One of the strengths of our discipleship ministry in Liberia is that we partner with the tSOAR ministry in Indianapolis. This ministry provides very generous financial support for our discipleship program, allowing us to provide refreshments at meetings, salary for our staff, and student scholarships.

Members of the discipleship program

Chapter 7: Entrepreneurship

Before describing CLTI's plan for entrepreneurship, I would like to describe how Yah's entrepreneurship experiences have helped our family.

Yah's Entrepreneurship

In 1982, my wife and I responded to God's call to pursue theological study to equip us for pastoral ministry. I was accepted into Africa Bible College (now Africa Bible College University) to pursue four years of study. Although we were blessed to obtain a scholarship from *Tear Fund Foundation* in the UK, the support went directly to the institution designated only for *tuition* expense, with no provision for food and other basic living expenses.

We had a two-year-old daughter (Lily) and three other siblings who had come to live with us (a total of six in our household). Soon after our studies began, we experienced a very difficult time securing an adequate food supply for our family. We started out very determined, but the expectation of continuing to the end of the 4-year program (without an adequate food supply) was unclear. It might not seem like much, but someone gave us a cash gift equivalent to $4.00 US! That night we kept praising the Lord for the gift and thanking the person who made the gift. I sat there thinking of the groceries we could purchase to last us for several weeks. Yah, however, reacted quickly by pointing out that once we had used the money to buy food, we would be back where we started and need to get additional funding repeatedly.

Yah came up with a wonderful, innovative idea. Yah said to me, "Tomorrow, I will follow the Christian ladies from the area market who go to the Liberian/Guinean border very early in the morning for goods. I could return by noon. With the Lord's help, I will use all the $4 gift to purchase fresh tomatoes, hot peppers, some grains, garden eggs, wildlife, pineapples, and any other food items that I could sell at my table."

I asked Yah, "Where did you get this idea, and how do you know it will work?" Then she explained, "I have been talking with several of the women in the market where I go to purchase food. They told me they get their supplies from the border and then sell them all afternoon. They also told me it was a profitable small business, and they encouraged me to start a business also."

The next morning, we prayed, and about 5:30 a.m. Yah took off for the border with the other business ladies. Using those $4 she purchased the marketable goods and within just two days all the items were sold! Yah continued with the profit to both purchase our groceries and additional groceries to sell in the local market.

The ladies had encouraged her in this business and Yah decided to expand the business by now purchasing 50- and 100-pound sacks of peppers, tomatoes and corn. This time, instead of selling retail by herself, she asked some of the women who were making the trip to Monrovia to sell her food items for a small commission. This worked well, too, and this "wholesale" enterprising idea helped other women by providing them with jobs.

CLTI's Entrepreneurship Program

The CLTI's entrepreneurship service was established in 2017. During our final ULICAF conference in Minnesota, some of Yah's friends gave her a gift of $700 and bid her farewell. Yah, instead of using the money on personal items, dedicated it to making loans to Liberian women, who though they didn't have resources, had job skills they had developed. This $700 gift started this loan program. We simply began by helping two young high school girls—Ruth and Lucia.

Ruth and Lucia came to see us for financial assistance. Lucia was a 12th grade student at a Catholic school in the city and Ruth was an 8th grade student at a local school. Both women visited us at different times and needed money for school tuition. We decided that rather than giving them a handout (which would help once but then need to be repeated) we would create a longer-term project to help them help themselves. If two people came every week, as they initially did, we would run out of funds very quickly.

So, we agreed to loan them $200 each to fund a *scratch card* phone business. These loans did not require collateral. They agreed to purchase scratch cards directly from the phone companies wholesale and then sell them at retail prices. Both women were given three months to pay back the loan. We set up a schedule to monitor them on a weekly basis. Prior to the end of the three months, Lucia came and paid off her loan. She also told us that she had paid off her school fees and purchased most of her personal needs. Ruth followed with a similar testimony. In a short time, a $400 investment had changed two lives and strengthened their faith in God.

You may be asking what scratch cards are. I should explain that the cell phone market in Liberia operates much differently than in the US. There are only two cell phone companies currently operating in Liberia. They are called "Orange" and "Lone Star." In Liberia a person does not purchase plans like those offered in America. To start, the person must purchase the phone. Phones range from $10.00 to $150.00 or more. The phones usually come from China and they are inexpensive. That is what most people can afford.

After purchasing the desired phone, the next step is to purchase a SIM card and you get a phone number with it. Then, you purchase *scratch cards*. These are your "minutes" of usage for the phone. The scratch cards are sold for one dollar and the minutes last for three days, and then you must get another card. Occasionally, the company would throw in a promotion that gives you an extension to 7 days total. These promotions are usually ongoing for about a month and are offered usually during a big holiday season like Christmas or New Year's. You can use a $2.00 "refill" which is applied for data for internet browsing.

The cell phone can be used to call almost everywhere in the fifteen counties in Liberia, except in very remote villages. The cell companies have built towers all over the country and particularly along the highways. There are a few places, like mountainous areas, where you might get poor reception or be unable to reliably connect.

Another exciting advantage of the cell phones in Liberia is that they allow you to transfer money from one city to another in just few seconds! You can go to any cell phone booth and transfer U.S. currency or local currencies for a small fee. Most cell phone users prefer making money transactions through the mobile transfer method rather than through the bank. Our office in Gompa pays our staff in Monrovia through mobile transfer every month, and we have had no problems.

So, back to Lucia and Ruth. After Lucia's and Ruth's success, the news spread quickly in the community. Small and non-business owners, mainly women, started visiting us and asking for small business loans.

From this point on, we realized the exciting potential of small businesses that could transform the lives of local Liberians. We knew that to make this successful we needed some strong supporters of this idea. Fortunately, a year prior to our experience with Lucia and Ruth, I had met a man from Columbus, Indiana, who for 10 years had been engaged in this kind of ministry business venture in Ghana, West

Africa. David Ketchum is the President and Founder of *Mission Resource International*. We reconnected and formed a partnership with his organization. His organization provided the first seed funds to expand the entrepreneurship loans to more women.

We also hired our first staff person who was directly responsible for overseeing the whole entrepreneurship ministry. She screened and conducted background checks and made recommendations of ladies she believed would potentially be successful with small business start-ups. The service is still ongoing.

Next Yah and I expanded the economic development loan ministry by launching our first satellite office in Monrovia in November 2019. That office, led by Priscilla Tuah, an African Bible College graduate who specialized in entrepreneurship, is focusing on three specific suburbs of Monrovia, the capital city of Liberia. We are very excited about the potential of helping many women in these suburban communities.

Our Gompa venture, though, remains our headquarters. Yah continues to lead this venture at the Gompa office, which is our one-stop clearing house for all information and resources pertaining to launching new business ventures other than selling SIM cards.

Yah and the entrepreneurial women

Chapter 8: Education Through After-School Outreach

Founded in September 2015, Christian Leadership Training International (CLTI) provides a tool for Yah and me to support leadership development for the people of Liberia. By focusing on discipleship, education, and entrepreneurship we hope to help our country. Of course, our involvement in leadership development didn't start in 2015. It began many years ago when God placed a call on the hearts of Yah and me to return to our home country and build Liberia International Christian College. LICC opened for its first students in March 2009, but the real work began many years earlier. The story and the working out of my vision truly began in 1997.

After choosing to answer God's call to give back to my native land, I enrolled in an Educational Leadership Policy Studies doctoral program at Loyola University Chicago. While there we had a burden to develop the future leaders of Liberia. This was the beginning of our story and the journey that commitment put us on, always continuing with our plans despite many tribulations and trials.

So, in 2014, Yah and I shifted our efforts entirely from college-age students (LICC) and focused on a younger generation of students. We had become troubled by the glaring failure rates for junior and senior high school students who were not able to pass the required high school and college entrance examinations. For example, it was not uncommon for only 5–10% to pass the West African Examination. Without a successful exam, these high school students would not be accepted into a college program. I had observed this academic problem with students who wanted to attend LICC but could not pass the state exam. Upon our arrival back in Liberia, we were determined to help empower students and prepare them to pass the college entrance examination.

First, we needed to understand why the majority of senior high students were failing the national examination. So, I invited the leaders of the Association of Christian Mission schools as well as the leaders of private schools from the various communities to meet with me to discuss the issues and come up with a solution openly and honestly. The majority answer was that the students, somehow, were not serious about their own lives and their studies. Another problem was the academic competency of the teachers themselves. Since the end of the 14–year civil war, the government has been unable to provide adequate training for teachers due to financial constraints. The teachers just did not understand the materials well themselves.

After several hours of discussion, I asked a second question, "What must we do to change this scenario?" I wanted to know what we could do as community leaders. There was then another long discussion, but this time I found a clue to the solution. First, the students were getting *less* instructional time than they did before the civil war. Some schools were running from 8:00 am to 12:00–12:30 pm. Most students were getting 4½ hours a day of class time, which was obviously not sufficient instructional time to prepare the students for the entrance exams or even to successfully understand the material at the next level.

One of the first CLTI projects was to launch an after-school training program for youth in the city of Gompa, the second largest commercial city in Liberia. For this program, I suggested three *additional* hours of after-school teaching daily, but the lessons would not be the regular classroom teachings they had received. The extra three hours daily would be *directly focused* on what the students needed to know to allow them to pass the national examination.

In the second meeting, we talked about a strategic plan for the program. The Association would identify the most competent teachers in any of the schools in Gompa to teach the following core courses: Chemistry, Physics, Biology, Math (Algebra and Trigonometry), Science, English, and Language Arts. They did identify 22 teachers, and I hired 18 of those 22.

Since we needed a location for the program, we were able to obtain the use of a Methodist high school campus. We chose the name *Reaching for Academic Excellence (RAE)*. We hired five monitors for all the classes. The monitors would be on campus fifteen minutes before all classes commenced. All classes would run from 3:00 pm to 6:00 pm, Monday through Thursday.

The academic period of instruction started four months prior to the state's date for the national examination. CLTI paid all the teachers and covered all the expenses for the materials. Each teacher would receive $65.00 which was more than what most teachers were paid for their full-time job. Teachers were banned from taking money from any of the students; if they took money, they would be dismissed. We offered the classes for free to all the students. We did not want the lack of finances to hold back any aspiring students. As funds were available, we would also provide snacks.

So in 2016, we launched *Reaching for Academic Excellence (RAE)*. Ten high schools joined the program and about 500 students enrolled. When the national test exam results came back, about 95% of the students passed the examination! The program had been a great success! In 2017, we repeated the program. This time, 12 high schools joined us, and more than 850 students enrolled. At the end of the program, more than 97% of students passed the examination, and Gompa came in first place in Nimba County. Through the program, students received academic tutoring, mentoring, and leadership coaching to encourage them in their education and in their walk with Christ.

Additionally, while this was going on, Yah was quite busy! CLTI, as I previously wrote, launched an entrepreneurship program to train, support, and empower women (many of whom are the sole supporters of their children and extended families) to start and grow their own small business. Yah and I experienced first-hand that as these women were encouraged to pursue their dreams (and provide for their families), this inspired their children to do the same. In 2017, over 27 loans were made to help start these small businesses. Popular ones were selling phone SIM cards and clothing.

Although *RAE* had been a success and we helped over 1000 students in 2 years, there were still some challenges. First, we had run out of space in the Methodist high school. We had maxed out the space with 60 students per classroom. Additionally, the intense afternoon heat became unbearable and made it difficult for the students to concentrate. So, for our third year, we had decided to try to find a larger facility that would be cooler during the heat of the afternoon. Unfortunately, we were unable to find such a facility locally at a price we could afford. We had to tentatively postpone the program until we could find or build a new facility.

Given these concerns and obstacles, we decided to search for land to build a school that would be adequate to serve all the *Reaching for Academic Excellence* program needs. We also had a comprehensive vision to build a large enough facility for a new high school.

Chapter 9: The New School

As we explained in Chapter 5, with God's help, we found five acres of land in a very strategic location. The location was less than two miles from the city center of Ganta and was on a main highway that will be paved soon. Through the generosity of American Christian friends and Liberian supporters, CLTI was able to purchase (and fully pay for) that beautiful piece of property.

We contracted EMI, an engineering ministry in the United States, to design the facility. On February 11, 2018, twelve members of the EMI project team travelled to Ganta to provide a conceptual design and master plan for the new campus. When the EMI team arrived, we explained our vision for the five-acre piece of land. It was to build a college preparatory high school for up to 2,000 students, a community medical clinic, and facilities to continue our entrepreneurship and discipleship programs.

EMI team members at work

The full EMI team

After EMI's review of the land, they saw that the sloping, uneven topography, and the steep ravine running through the middle of the site, drastically reduced the usable land area on which buildings could be constructed. As a result of these site challenges, their conceptual design package proposed a school campus that will accommodate a reduced number of 1,200–1,500 students, while still maintaining the medical clinic and entrepreneurship and discipleship components of the vision. A preliminary cost estimate for the full build-out of the entire campus, as shown in the master plan, was just over $3 million.

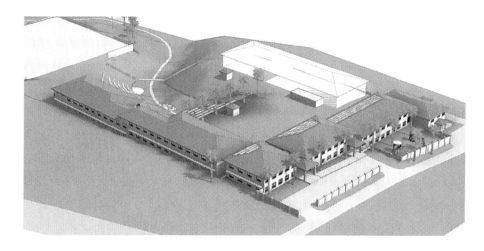

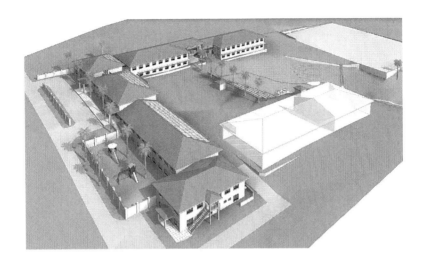

Once the facility's plan was complete, we moved forward with the construction. We hired a construction engineer who is a young, bright, and dedicated Ghanaian; a project manager; and an accountant, two of whom were graduates of LICC, the college we helped to establish. Yah and I joined the team, and we launched the groundbreaking on May 19, 2018. We were blessed to have a friend, Jay Skinner, from Indianapolis, join us during the groundbreaking ceremony. Before his return, I had a great conversation with Jay about his own perspective about the new vision. He was electrified by the goals and vision we had for this school. He committed to generous financial giving and to networking as well among his friends in the United States to help us raise support.

Following the groundbreaking, I wrote the county government, asking for a yellow machine (a local term for an earthmover) to clear and level the ground as the site was so very sloped. But, before the county machine could get ready to help, a private machine operator heard about our need. He proposed that in exchange for leveling and preparing the site that we would give him dirt that he needed. We agreed, and the "yellow machine" arrived, and did more work than we could have anticipated!

Once the site was cleared and leveled, and all the other ground preparation was behind us, the next task was building a foundation. On August 19, 2018, we commenced digging the foundation *by hand* (47 daily workers helped us). See the pictures on pages 52 and 53. This was a blessing to the local population that needed work. While the digging progressed, we began making our own bricks and molded 15,000 bricks of two different sizes (eight-inch and six-inch bricks).

To make bricks, we needed cement. We asked our ministry partners to donate to cover the cost of a certain number of sacks of cement and the labor cost to make a specific number of bricks. In this way, supporters could see how their donations were building the school brick by brick!

From August 19, 2018, through January 2022, we completed the foundation, laid the foundation slab and built the first-floor walls.

Transporting bags of cement

Casting the foundation

Right now, as I am writing, the first building is complete, short of few details such as painting, a few windows, and a science lab. Classes are ongoing in this current building. We have drilled a well for clean drinking water. We have designated an acre and started growing various fruit trees—oranges, avocados, mangos, and coconuts. We are also raising pigs, and constructing a cafeteria which is at a roof level.

If you wonder why the foundation is so tall in the photo, it is because it includes an apartment. The ground was sloped steeply at one end of the building. Instead of filling it in, our project manager came up with the idea of adding a small walk-out basement apartment. The apartment will provide accommodation for four visiting instructional staff or two couples who come to teach for RICA on a short-term basis.

Foundation and first floor in progress

When we started the second floor, we had to first *cast* the floor. We needed corrugated steel and wood and steel bar to strengthen it. Also, we put in electric wiring and all the plumbing before we cast the cement floor.

Once we had the floor finished, we could then put up the second-floor walls. This process was much like the first floor, except that the construction materials had to be lifted from the ground floor to the second floor. Most of the lifting was by hand. Imagine the effort that strong young men had to exert while climbing ladders carrying cement bricks and other construction materials.

To make wise use of our funds, we decided to put floor tiles only in the bathrooms and administration areas. For the classrooms we hired skilled craftsmen who just used smooth cement for the floors.

Once the basic cement walls were built, it was time for plastering. In this process, the young workers laid thin layers of cement over the brick walls. The desired result is a smooth wall that eventually will be painted.

When we had the second story built, it was time to start on the roof. We used corrugated sheet metal which most large commercial buildings in Liberia use.

We first had to build the frame that would support the metal roof. This required getting termite-free wood which is very expensive. We needed boards in a number of sizes, including 2" x 2", 2" x 4", 2" x 6", 2" x 8" boards. These boards were cut to the right lengths and fastened together with nails.

Once the frame was in place, we were ready for our sheet metal. We hoped to be able to afford one of the better qualities of sheet metal. The metal is coated with zinc to make it rust-free, and the better grades have a better coating as well. It costs about $150 a bundle of twenty 8' x 4' sheets. Fortunately, with our large roof, we were able to buy in bulk and get a cheaper price. It took 93 bundles to cover the whole building. Besides the metal sheets, we needed special zinc nails to attach the sheets to our wood frame.

We found out that a special skill is needed to build stairs of cement and steel that appear like nothing is holding it up. But then the result is beautiful and practical.

We had learned building skills from the development of LICC. We also learned to build in stages. We trusted God for the finances and built one floor at a time. We did not want to be in debt when we finished the building. To help make the construction process a visual reality to our ministry partners we displayed our "stages" of finished construction on our website and in our newsletters. In this way, they could see how they directly impacted the building of the school.

For example:

> "A donation of $10 will buy one bag of concrete. This concrete is needed for our next project of applying the exterior and interior finish coat to the walls. A donation of $100 will help us purchase a window or door. Each donation will help us reach our goal to build the first college preparatory high school in Liberia. Your donation is so much appreciated!"

We used similar requests for the foundation (money for bags of cement, bricks, steel, and wood), walls (money for bags of cement for bricks, mainly), and roof (money for corrugated metal and wood).

We also highlighted the larger stages. For example, one program was Project 90/150. We were looking for 90 donations of $150. That would be enough to buy the metal for the roof. Occasionally we are blessed to have large donations, but mostly we get smaller donations. A request for them might be:

> "If you have the means, or if you could join with family members or friends to donate $150 for a bundle of roofing, your donation will bring so much to the people of Liberia. It will bring future nurses, future doctors, and other health care professionals to Liberia, which is lacking in medical care. It is so much more than simply a roof over the heads of students and teachers. It is hope for the future."

For plastering:

> "The ground floor plastering is 70% complete. This means we are only 30% away from completing the ground floor plastering and will now start on the second-floor plastering. Twelve extremely skillful concrete masons are pressing on toward the finish line!
>
> Some of the work teams have already started the exterior plastering. Unfortunately, we are out of material. 1,000 bags of cement are still needed to complete the entire plastering job—inside and outside. Today, would you please consider donating to allow us to purchase more bags of cement?
>
> $100 will purchase ten bags of cement. Thirty bags of cement will complete one whole classroom. $5,000 will purchase 700 bags direct from the cement factory in Monrovia at wholesale price and complete the entire ground floor and most of the second floor!"

My friends ask what it is like to start again, after constructing LICC. I explain to them the benefit of the prior experience. It is a different school with a new set of challenges, but the basics are the same. Assuming God provides the resources, I am expecting to make faster progress than we made with LICC. Additionally, God has brought in more generous partners than we had ever expected or imagined.

In Luke 14:28, Jesus gave a parable in which He emphasized the wisdom of counting the cost of your goal: if you don't finish, you will be openly saying to everyone in town how you foolishly didn't plan well. For this reason, we continue to build in stages and now are forging ahead to the finish line. We officially opened the school on November 1, 2021, and invited friends, donors and our community leaders to a fabulous celebration!

My favorite picture of RICA--with students in the yard!

Chapter 10: More Than a Building

We have finally constructed a state-of-the-art school facility which is now fully functioning. We have furnished the building with computers, both in offices and the computer lab; a fully stocked library (shelves and books on many subjects at all grade levels); and chairs and desks. Besides those physical needs, we have developed the curriculum, registered with the government, recruited staff, and enrolled more than 400 students from grade one through twelve, and hired 32 instructional staff.

Furniture

As I write this, we have been blessed with donations of huge shipments of furniture provided by Santa Barbara Community Church in California and Westfield High School in Indiana.

Thanks to the dedication of one of our partner churches, we received two 40−foot shipping containers filled with elementary and high school furnishings. Kevin Callaway and members of the Santa Barbara Community gathered 35 boxes of elementary textbooks, 20 boxes of high school textbooks, general reading and research books, art supplies, white boards, 10 office desks, library tables and chairs, sporting equipment and high school science equipment! We are so grateful to our friends in Santa Barbara, California.

Prior to our arrival in the United States, we had a board meeting via teleconference in September. During the meeting the board asked each team member to send a letter to local schools in their respective area to encourage them to give furniture for the new school. Jon Lieberman, our board chairman, sent his letter to Mayor Andy Cook of Westfield.

For the Westfield donation, here is a word from Jon:

"I sent it to the Mayor of Westfield who instructed the head of the schools to talk with me. Westfield High School is remodeling their whole school and now will provide us with desks, chairs, whiteboards, bookshelves, etc. Westfield gave us 9 library chairs, an assortment of tables, 13 metal single desks, 240 sled desks and green metal chairs, 35 wooden chairs, 24 chalk and white boards, and 20 teacher desks!

We are so grateful for a church and a local high school that caught the vision, not just for resources to help their own community, but really saw the vital need for educating children in a third-world country.

Curriculum

We also needed a curriculum. This is a great academic challenge—to have the physical resources and, most importantly, the human resources to develop the courses for many grade levels and to hire competent staff as administrators, teachers, and support and maintenance personnel.

We have produced comprehensive Student and Teacher Handbooks which will be a guide for practical management purposes as well as an ethical, biblically–based guide for student behavior. Our original intent was to start the school with grades seven through twelve.

For a school to register with the Liberian government, Liberia's national school standards have to be satisfied. The Liberian government provides basic curriculum requirements that must be met. We are a Liberian school, so the basic foundation of the curriculum that will be taught is based on our country's requirements. For that purpose, we used a team of teachers and administrators on the ground along with two friends from Santa Barbara, California who helped to align the curriculum. They reviewed the basic Liberia National Educational Standards and the more general STEAM (Science, Technology,

Engineering, Art, and Math) curriculum as core classes. We understand also that learning is not just about memorizing facts, but also being able to do critical thinking and solve problems. We are not losing sight of the goal of preparing them to take the Liberian National Exam.

The school's focus is based on STEAM. While there are some basic STEAM requirements in the national educational requirements, we planned and added a much more extensive curriculum so that our students will have the academic training to attend not only a university in Liberia but be qualified and prepared to study abroad. For example, if a student wants to go to graduate school to be a Physician Assistant, or even a medical doctor, we want to give them enough science courses to prepare them for such a career.

I sometimes give my experience with typing as an example of adjusting to changing technology. I was trained traditionally in Africa to use all my fingers and to type quickly. Our goal was 60 words per minute. I didn't see a computer until I came to America in 1994. A computer may function completely differently from a typewriter, but it has the same keyboard. It took me a while to learn to use the computer (like remembering to save frequently so I wouldn't lose my work!). However, I had an advantage over some of my classmates because I had been taught to touch–type.

The A in STEAM is Important

We are fortunate to have a container coming from friends in California with art supplies (crayons, pencils, paper, markers, etc.). We consider this initial form of self-expression a very important aspect of communicating.

We needed a drawing of the ground-level apartment in our building and gave the project to a high school student. He was unable to draw a simple floor plan—a porch outside, two bedrooms, and one bathroom. Our engineer (from Ghana) was able to draw the plan in a few minutes.

Is being able to draw a useful life skill? In some professions it is. For this reason, we are hoping to include art classes in the curriculum of our school.

Liberian students learn to read and write in English in school. Often, the reading and writing level is very basic. To enhance their skills, we want to get them writing and learning the principles of research from the beginning. In Liberia, academic writing usually begins in the Junior or Senior years of high school. (This problem of not including it in early learning is because of too few teachers available to review all these papers.)

In Liberia today, our economy sells raw materials abroad while needing to import finished items. Even much of our food is imported. We anticipate as the economy develops and becomes more modern, our students will need to be prepared and trained to get jobs in these careers. We are already planning for this type of advanced training.

For example, years ago our spiritual daughter came to live with us in Noblesville, Indiana. We took her to obtain a driver's license in Noblesville. She had arrived in America a short time prior from Liberia. She was also a college student in sociology from the University of Liberia. So, the lady processing the license asked a basic question, "What is your height?" She could not give the correct answer, and instead she remained very quiet and looked at me for help.

Today, that same young woman is among the brightest in our Liberian community in Indianapolis. She has obtained an Associate Degree in Medical Information and is now working for a reputable company in Indianapolis, Indiana. (She also achieved her American dream two years ago by purchasing her own house!) Currently, she is planning to

86

pursue another professional degree in Cancer Information Technology. I am very proud of this young woman.

I would like to discuss one criticism of African education that we are looking to address at our school. In many African schools, there is book learning, but not much hands-on or practical training. For example, students may study the chemistry book, but not have a chance to do laboratory work to see some of what they are learning or have learned put into practice. Like with the writing lessons, often the issue is lack of teaching time. Also, in case of science lab work, the school must have the facilities to conduct the labs. That can be a difficult issue because we feel fortunate to just have a basic classroom.

Teachers and Staff

We try to make wise decisions in recruiting teachers. We pursue Godly individuals who are trained to teach our specialized curriculum.

Prior to developing the college preparatory high school, we developed an *after-school* student program designed to tutor high school students before they took their state examination called *Reaching for Academic Excellence*. We needed highly qualified teachers in the areas of biology, math, chemistry, physics, and economics to prepare the students to pass the state exam. To develop the curriculum, we sent someone to Monrovia to buy *sample* tests for the last 5+ years. In the US students buy manuals such as "Preparing to take the SATs" that have hundreds of sample questions.

We then hired several instructors and discussed the best ways to cover the material. Although there were minor changes between each edition of the test, once we had the basics, we could use the same material for the second year.

We have developed the school curriculum in a similar way. Each year we will need an ongoing supply of quality teachers to teach the curriculum.

As we develop our staff, we will be conscious of the need to have diversity in the background of the teachers. In our country diversity applies to one's tribal background. Diversity, unlike in America, is not about skin color or race. For example, my tribe is *Mano*. Liberians have a natural pride in their specific tribal background, heritage and customs. We want to foster an inter-tribal network of teachers representing as many different cultures as we can. We will still focus on the character and academic training of each teacher.

For example, our school is being built by a young but very bright and competent engineer from Ghana. The facility was designed by Engineering Ministries International (American engineers). The structural work was done by a professor from the Engineering Department of the University of Liberia. We used Liberian-made concrete bricks. We hired Liberians from various tribal groups to construct the building. Each individual brought their talents, expertise and experience.

As we have talked to administrators at other schools about staff, we have learned about different leadership styles based on one's culture. Originally, we had planned to have up to 3 or 4 principals—one each for elementary, middle and high schools. However, in talking to other principals and administrators, they suggested this could result in a fight for power between the different grades. So instead, we are looking at one principal for the whole school. Additionally, we would also hire a vice principal for instruction to monitor all teaching staff, and a dean of students to supervise the students and provide discipline as needed.

I observed a Catholic high school of 600 students in Liberia. When lunch time was over and the bell rang, all the students were back in their respective classes before the second bell rang. It was extremely impressive. We hope to have similar discipline for the teachers and students. I include teachers because they will set the example for the students.

When we opened, we had around 20 teachers, and as of this writing, there are around 30 teachers. We currently have a Principal, a Business Manager, Vice Principal for Instruction who monitors the teachers, Vice Principal for Administration, and Math and Science department heads to ensure the school runs well. We need to always remember that this school is much more than just a building.

In working with our American friends, we have become convinced that it is important to support the teachers to ensure they are doing all they can to help the students learn the material. We hope to mentor, train, and monitor our teachers. They need to not only know the material they will teach and also know how to teach it, but they need to understand how to teach a whole lesson in a class period, so that the students can go on to the next lesson during the next class. We need to help them avoid taking shortcuts in implementation and make sure subjects are being covered fully. Our goal is to align with international standards. We are hoping to get visiting teams to help us with this effort.

Support Staff – Custodians

There are many parts of running a school. One practical aspect is figuring out who will clean the school. Due partly to a lack of jobs in the area during the building of our main building, a number of women came to help at the construction site. These women drew water (for making cement), carried sand, moved bricks, etc. These small jobs provided the women with money to care for their children and provided us with reliable labor to help with construction. Now that construction is mostly complete on the main building, we have less need for their help. Fortunately, since jobs are still scarce in the area, we were able to hire some of the women (7 or 8) to clean the school each morning. It would have been nice to hire all of them, but some of the women will be employed again as we start construction on our next buildings. Creating jobs is another way we can help the local economy.

Support Staff – Groundskeeper

Our original conceptual landscape design was by EMI volunteers from Nigeria. A landscape designer from Nigeria has helped us prepare the detailed design. She spent 2 months laying out trees, grass, and roundabouts.

During a trip to Ghana and Monrovia we saw different trees for sale. We got some Royal Palms. We are hoping to have a fruit farm with over 150 trees, including coconuts, mangos, oranges, avocado (butter pear), plantains, and bananas. Most, like coconut trees, will take a number of years of growth before they bear fruit, but they are an investment in our future.

Unfortunately, after planting we were hit by a heat wave, so some will need to be replanted. Hopefully, by replanting in May 2023, the trees will have enough time to root before the next dry season hits.

Our groundskeeper will be the one trying to keep the campus beautiful, but also supporting efforts like our fruit farm to build sustainability for RICA.

Chapter 11: Why? The Children

Our original plan was to open in 2020; however, with COVID-19 restrictions, we postponed the date to November of 2021. Our neighbors expectantly watched the progress of the construction and waited patiently for the completion and opening of the school. When I say neighbors, I am not just talking about adults and local officials, but the children as well!

In America and Europe, almost all children have access to education, even if some don't want to take advantage of their opportunity! It's not that way in Liberia. Many children have no access locally for a quality education. They know that a Christ-centered education will lead to a better life for themselves and their families. Not long ago, several boys visited the construction site. I thought perhaps they had come to ask for food. They noted how the building exterior was almost complete and with faces of excitement asked when it would open. I had to tell them of the delay due to COVID-19. I prayed with the boys, and we all prayed together for the completion of the school.

You might ask, "So, why aren't these boys and girls attending school classes?" First, there is a real need for more schools to accommodate the many children in the community. Second, even if there were additional schools, many children would still need financial assistance even with the low tuition fees we charge.

For example, I recently learned about the hardship circumstances of one of the boys. His mother had died in childbirth. His father does not have a job. He had a massive stroke which left one side of his body paralyzed. He drags himself from house-to-house looking for odd jobs and for food. Not all of our students will come from such impoverished circumstances, but many will have very real financial struggles.

In one of our recent newsletters, we shared the struggles of these boys who came to visit the construction site. Several people requested updates on the status of these boys. Two of our friends from Santa Barbara Community Church in California provided sponsorships for two of the boys.

Opening Day

Hopefully, those who have read this far have an appreciation for all the work that goes into starting a new school. On Monday, November 1, 2021, we opened the school for orientation and registration. Although it took several days to process them, we started with 440 students. That meant that 440 young Liberians have the opportunity to be learning things that will give them a brighter future.

Registration on November 1, 2021

Although, I experienced the opening of Liberia International Christian College so many years ago now, it still was an amazing day for me. It was an amazing day for students who, for the first time, moved freely through our hallways, finding their classroom—hoping to share a room with their friends.

Students wearing their uniforms assemble for morning devotions

Morning Assembly in front of school

Older students in classroom

Younger students visiting while waiting for class to start

Part 3

The Future of RICA

Chapter 12: What Comes Next?

Completing the Physical Plant of Our First Building

We have a building, but to have a functioning, operational school we need **water** for the bathrooms and drinking. We worked with Living Water International (www.water.cc) to drill a deep borehole to obtain a reliable, continual source of good drinking water. We needed to drill 250 feet to get clean water and that cannot be done by hand. Living Water International has the machinery to create such a well.

We also needed **electricity** to run the computers and office equipment and provide adequate lighting for the building and classrooms. There is a private utility company in the city, and we worked with them and purchased electricity.

Our initial focus was on finishing the classrooms and restrooms. To open the school, those needed to be usable for the students and teachers. We were still working on the administrative areas of the school (e.g., offices for administrators, a room for student records, etc.) because we didn't need those to be fully complete when classes started. Initially, we didn't have enough furniture to fill all the classrooms, so we used unfurnished classrooms for administration and also as a cafeteria.

The **cafeteria** is important because most RICA students cannot afford breakfast at home before heading to school. Our recess (or meal-time) starts early at 11:00 or 11:30 am. The price of the food ranges from 100–200 Liberian dollars (about $0.70–$1.40 U.S.). What do we feed them? The staple food in Liberia is rice. In Nimba County, the staple is two-fold: rice and cassava (a tuber that grows underground like a potato). Various types of grains, beans, or cooked leaves are used for the sauce. The grains are boiled, fried in vegetable oil or palm oil, or steamed. There is also hot pepper soup. At other times, the students would be provided spaghetti, popcorn, cassava, or sweet potatoes. When meat is available, it is primarily fish.

Additional Buildings

For the cafeteria, we have what we call Phase II. We are constructing a second building that will house the cafeteria, gym and chapel. This building will be approximately half the size of our original classroom–administration building. The contractor commenced the construction task in February 2022. Although initially we used a classroom for a cafeteria (it did work very well for this purpose), we found we could only serve a limited number of students at a time, so we had multiple lunch times, and that made class scheduling difficult. Also, we needed to use the classrooms for classes. Like our original building, we had the conceptual design completed by the American volunteer group EMI; an American friend who is an architect did the detailed design; and a local construction company is supervising construction.

Special guests join us for cafeteria groundbreaking

Cafeteria building groundbreaking

Riverview cafeteria foundation

99

As of June 2, 2023, the building housing the cafeteria, gym, and chapel is roofed

Elementary School and Healthcare Building

God-willing, Phase III of the building plan will give us an elementary school and healthcare building. Before that is completed, we are using one classroom for a clinic, hopefully with a registered nurse. This provides healthcare for teachers and students.

Clinic in classroom with nurse's desk and shelves of medicines

Administrative Area

For the administrative area, we needed to put window bars on to protect important administrative documents and finances. We needed certain types of protection that weren't necessary for classrooms.

More Land

As I mentioned earlier, we had several options for land when choosing a location for the school. We chose what we felt was the best location even though we knew we might have to scale back plans for building because of the relatively small size of the plot.

The good news is we have been able to buy other small plots of land adjoining our land, but purchasing some of the plots required creative solutions. For example, one family would have sold us their mud house and plot of land if we would have built them a mud house in a different location. Unfortunately, we didn't have the money for that arrangement. Yet, God has provided. Currently we have 7.24 acres and will buy more adjoining land as finances allow!

Sustainability

Sustainability is the reason some of the campus area has fishponds, fruit trees, and pigs. The fish, fruit, and pork are things we can sell for money to support the operation of the school as well as using them to feed our students and teachers. Some of this will take time. It takes several years for fruit trees to bear fruit. All the while they must be cared for and some won't survive.

In the case of fish, we are now on our second batch. For our initial batch of tilapia, we dug ponds and got starter fish from local women. They grew and multiplied and multiplied again when we didn't harvest them during the COVID-19 year. However, they never grew very large. We knew we needed to do better.

Learning is the important thing in all subjects. Since that first harvest of small fish, I have gotten some assistance from "teachers" of raising tilapia. For this next batch we are getting the female and male fish from farms who raise baby fish. There is more cost involved, but the fish are bred to grow larger. Hopefully, the results of that will be seen in our next harvest.

RICA fish ponds with RICA in background

Our first harvest of fish

When I was in the United States learning how to start schools, I didn't give much thought to how important understanding agriculture would be. Today I am not just a "fisher of men," but a "fisher of fish," too.

Another part of sustainability is establishing the right cost of tuition for the students. We seek to balance the cost of running a school with the limited funds of most our students' families. We considered that when we set our tuition. So far, we have been fortunate that most (85–90%) have been able to pay their school fee. Of course, we will try to find assistance for those who can't. We are hoping that over the long term, the cost of the staff can be covered by tuition.

To encourage sustainability, we have avoided the traditional approach—"they are poor, let it be free." It sounds good, but I have found that it is impossible for the school to hire good teachers who can work for free! The trained chemistry teacher, for example, wants or needs to be paid for their time. Yes, many of our students will be poor.

So, we try to balance the need for students and their families to recognize the value of what they receive but also make it affordable.

As part of this, we believe that if we are choosing the right godly students, over the years, some part of our community will be blessed and transformed. As that occurs, hopefully, we will be able to raise enough income to keep our instruction going at a high standard. If we are just mediocre this won't happen.

First seniors to graduate November 23, 2023

As students get a better education and even a college education, we feel that some the of their resultant prosperity will find its way back into the project to pay competent staff and good teachers, to subsidize what is earned from student tuition, and to provide sponsorships for students who can contribute little if anything.

We appreciate all the donations we have received so far. We know that we will need additional monies to finally get the school to a fully functioning level. But, to enable the school to last from generation to generation the school needs to make itself sustainable.

The Community

A famous Bangladeshi social entrepreneur and founder of the Grameen Bank, Muhammad Yunus, taught the principles of how to successfully run an organization as a social business. The goal of the organization should be more than just to make money. What the organization does (like a school) should help the community in as many ways as possible. What motivates people to work, to study, to face challenges? To have a better life for themselves? To right some great wrong? Revenge? Love? For many people, those are motivations. Some other people are focused on helping change people's lives. Let me tell you the story of one of those people.

There was "a bush boy" who didn't own a pair of shoes or "officially" start school until he was 10. A missionary came to his village when he was in high school and helped him find God and accept Christ. He made a decision to focus on his education to get out of poverty. The boy pursued education at great cost, working at whatever job or business he could, travelling to foreign countries, if necessary, to improve himself and provide for others.

It is an amazing story, one of adventure, heartache, and sacrifice. But it is a real story of the life of a bush boy. I know it can happen, and I know it happens—because it happened to me. I detailed my early life in my first book, *No More War*. I have had a better life because I took my lifelong passion for education and dedication to Jesus (once I became a Christian) to help other people. My passion was not just to help me. My passion was not just to help my family, although I care for them dearly. I have spent my life pursuing my passion of building and equipping schools for my fellow Liberians so that they might have a better life.

And the story is not just about the students. It doesn't do any good to educate students unless they can go out and help others, too. Now that I am back in Liberia, I want to help my community with the resources and education I received. For example, why does a school need a fish farm or a fruit farm? Part of it is sustainability for the school. However, it is not just about the school's sustainability. I want to help the local community have access to higher quality food at reasonable prices. In the spirit of social business, we are trying to build and run a school and help the community all at the same time.

When we build with local labor, does it help the local community? Yes, the laborers are able to provide for their families. When teachers are paid on time at the end of each month, it is a beautiful thing for the community. The teachers benefit from being paid, but the community does as well when the teachers buy local goods like food. Some of the teachers even come from Monrovia and rent houses from local people, helping the local economy. The government gets taxes, as social security is paid for each employee (4% by employees and 6% by employers) to help provide for our employees' futures. We want the school's success to be a win-win situation for the local community and, in some small way, for Liberia as a whole.

Chapter 13: Future Vision for Our High School

So, I have embarked on this new adventure, and just like with LICC, not knowing where it will lead, but trusting God, I once again believe that God has amazing plans for this school.

The school will not only serve as a college preparatory high school in the city of Gompa, but we still intend to serve *all* the high schools in Gompa and *all* of their senior high students in our after-school study program *Reaching for Academic Excellence*. In November of 2021, Riverview International Christian Academy launched its regular classes from grade one to grade twelve and enrolled 440 students!

There is a wonderful history connected with the land upon which The Riverview International Christian Academy (RICA) was built. Friends have asked me why the name Riverview was chosen. They asked if there was a river nearby. The answer is "No."

The river is about 10 miles away from the school. "Yarsonnoh," the village of my birth, is located at the very edge of the river Yar. The name of the village, "Yarsonnoh," is translated "village beside the river." The Yar River is the source of life for all the inhabitants of this small village for fresh drinking water, cooking, bathing, and fish for food. Symbolically, RICA, like Yar River, will serve as *the source of life* to educate, train, equip, nurture, and disciple for Jesus every student that attends the school. There is no doubt that over time, RICA will be the epicenter of major positive changes in the surrounding area.

RICA's original five acres has expanded and is being developed. When we first walked there, the land was overgrown with bushes and weeds that we painstakingly cleared so we could lay the foundation of the first building on the property. We are hopeful about the future impact of the school where a student's whole extended family can rejoice over the miracle of RICA and the opportunity of an education that didn't exist before.

We marvel at what God has done. In place of a desolate undeveloped piece of land, we now are growing fish in ponds, raising pigs, planting figs and other fruit trees and providing honey from bees! Where there was only grass, classrooms now will be filled with children who will become Liberia's future leaders.

We have been diligently working over these last six years to develop this property, but we know this is only the beginning. I am reminded of Paul's encouraging words, "I am confident that He who began a good work here will indeed carry it to completion" (Phil. 1:6) and that students would know that their lives in the Lord had a great beginning at RICA and the school's impact will continue until the day that Jesus returns. We anticipate that many lives will be transformed and whole families' lives will be improved which will revolutionize our local Gompa community and Nimba County.

We will teach students to pursue academic excellence, to think creatively, and to be problem solvers. We will teach them that all people are created in God's image with purpose and importance. Most of all, we will teach them that they are valued, cherished, and adored by the Lord Jesus. We expect many students to emerge as leaders for peace and true social justice in communities throughout Liberia—which can only be accomplished through faith in Jesus.

Recently, I had the opportunity to meet with a long-term generous supporter and share more details about RCA and our vision to impact our nation. After sharing our vision, my friend put his hands in his pocket and pulled out a check from his wallet. It was a check for $25,000! I promised my friend that his gift would provide pure drinking water for all our students and staff for about 25 years. We then began negotiating with Living Water International to drill a well about 250 feet deep. A portion of the gift will be used to underwrite seven hundred bags of cement that we need to complete the interior, exterior, and flooring of the building.

The expanded campus space will include an elementary school and health center. Currently, the junior and senior high facility has been constructed, but is being used for grades one through twelve. We are using classrooms in it for the library, cafeteria, a health center, and computer lab. The building that will house the cafeteria, gym and chapel is under construction. The soccer field and an administrative building are in the process of being completed. We have space also designated for CLTI's current after-school program, as well as for outdoor recreation as God provides the resources. Additionally, our plans include a self-contained fish and agricultural system, which are being implemented piece by piece. This system is to provide the campus with a sustainable source of revenue through the production of vegetables, fruit and fresh fish.

We will have an entrepreneurship and discipleship center for Christian Leadership Training International to hold meetings and instructional space for workshops, small group meetings, and other adult opportunities for continuing education.

The proposed community medical clinic will serve as an outpatient day clinic and will be equipped with examination rooms, laboratory space, procedure rooms, a day-ward, and a pharmacy. We plan to have a "school nurse" for our students, but the clinic will allow/extend medical support to the local community.

Part 4

A New Perspective

Chapter 14: Looking Back

If you were to ask me how I dealt with my departure from LICC some years back, I would say I knew that it was most important to move on. I wanted to put the past behind me; however, as my new mission began to take shape, I now have had some time to reflect on what had really happened when I left ULICAF and LICC.

I will start by discussing some prior conflicts and tension that existed among some key staff members. Conflicts created by different approaches to solving problems and different ideas on creating a viable ministry organization are inevitable, but they don't have to ruin a ministry. They can be beneficial to finding a better way of doing ministry if everyone will pray, corporately seek God together, and give up their own self-seeking plans. Biblical history gives us many examples of family conflicts.

The patriarch Abraham and his extended family give us a glimpse into a family that suffered family feuds. Some of their personal choices led to conflicts that still exist and affect the world today! Personal conflict in the Bible goes all the way back to the first man, Adam, and his family.

- **Adam accused Eve of being his own tempter and the cause of his own choices**. "The woman you put here with me—she gave me some fruit from the tree, and I ate it." (Gen. 3:12 NIV).

- **First conflict and murder occurred in the very first family.** Most readers are familiar with the tragic biblical account of the jealousy Cain had toward Abel. Adam and Eve gave birth to two sons—Cain and Abel. Each son had a different occupation. Abel was a keeper of a sheep. Cain was a tiller of the ground.

- **Cain killed his little brother because he was *jealous*.** The LORD looked with favor on Abel and his offering, but on Cain and his offering he did not look with favor. So, Cain was very angry, and his face was downcast. (Gen. 4:4−5 NIV)

- **Joseph's brother sold him in Egypt due to *favoritism* that Jacob showed Joseph over his brothers.** "Now Israel loved Joseph more than any of his other sons, because he had been born to him in his old age; and he made an ornate robe for him. When his brothers saw that their father loved him more than any of them, they hated him and could not speak a kind word to him." (Gen. 37:3−4 NIV)

- **Rebekah favored Jacob, and Jacob *cheated* Esau.** "Esau held a grudge against Jacob because of the blessing his father had given him. He said to himself, 'The days of mourning for my father are near; then I will kill my brother Jacob.'" (Gen. 27:41 NIV)

God did not favor one career *calling* over another, but biblical scholars believe that God was more concerned about the *attitude* that the worshipper had while presenting their offering. Abel, the text says, offered the "fat portions of the firstborn of his flock" (Gen.4:4 NIV) indicating that they were some of the best animals in his flock. The text is not exactly clear why God did not look with favor on Cain's offering, but we can guess that he didn't bring the best of his crops or that he disobeyed some instruction regarding the offering.

Cain, rather than repenting for his sinful attitude (disobedience) turned his feelings of rejection into an evil attitude of hostility toward Abel whose offering God did favor and killed his brother! (See 1 John 3:12)

God reminded Cain that if he had obeyed God ("done what was right" – Gen. 4:7 NIV), his offering would have been accepted. It wasn't personal preference on God's part, or disdain for Cain's vocation, or the quality of his produce that caused God to reject his sacrifice. God told Cain, "Sin lies crouching at the door," (Gen. 4:7 NIV) waiting to pounce like a lion, so it would fulfill its desire to overpower him.

What do we learn from this? Cain allowed sin to rule over him, and consequently, God placed a curse on Cain and all his life he would be a wanderer, "a fugitive and a vagabond" (Gen. 4:12, 24 NIV). Unresolved, any conflict can create an offended party (rightly or wrongly offended) who can have a jealous, angry, "murderous" spirit that can, and often does, cause one to slander another.

Conflict in the Early Church

The prior biblical examples and narratives were taken from the Old Testament Scriptures. But in the very beginnings of a Holy Spirit-filled church, could conflicts arise?

God blessed the early Church, and their numbers were steadily growing. Then there arose a dispute over food distribution as the widows were neglected. The Hellenist (Greek) believers complained that their widows were not receiving an adequate share of the food the Church provided for the care of other of the ethnic Hebrew-speaking widows. (see Acts 6:1)

Later there was division in the church at Corinth (see I Cor. 3:1–23). A conflict arose around the issue of who were the true apostles and disciples. Paul reasoned with them, telling them that their factionalism did not come from the Spirit, but from their pride and arrogance of being in the "special group that believed in Jesus."

115

Some claimed to belong to Paul while others claimed to belong to Apollo's sect. Various people followed different leaders as they all claimed to believe in Jesus. This situation led to chaos and was a bad testimony to outsiders. Paul used the word "carnal" and considered it to be the root cause of the conflict among this group of believers.

Though all believers have the Holy Spirit, they still struggle with various temptations that arise from their own self and sinful nature (see Romans 7:14–25). Followers of Jesus are called to grow in spiritual maturity which will ultimately reveal our human faults and sins. If these character flaws are left unresolved, they lead to a host of non-Christian attitudes and choices: envy, coveting, lying, anger, etc. which lead to strife and broken relationships. When this happens brothers and sisters stop really listening to one another, which leads to unresolved conflicts. Instead of being marked by our "love for one another," (see John 13:35) an unbelieving world sees our disunity in the body of Christ. It hurts the cause of evangelism and discourages Christians in their pursuit of God.

Two Best Friends Go Separate Ways

Barnabas was a leading foundational Jewish leader among the early Apostles. After Paul (Saul of Tarsus) encountered his Jewish Messiah Jesus as a young Rabbi, Barnabas took him and introduced him to the rest of the Apostles and helped Paul on his first successful missionary journey which began by traveling to the island of Cyprus.

However, on one of Paul and Barnabas's journeys, a young man named John Mark, a cousin of Barnabas, accompanied them to Antioch (see Acts 12:25), and later to Cyprus (see Acts 13:4–5). For an unknown reason, Mark deserted Paul and Barnabas in a city called Perga (see Acts 13:13).

On the next opportunity to minister, Mark wanted to come along again, but Paul refused to take Mark because of his previous desertion (see Acts 15:36–41). This created a sharp division between Barnabas and Paul and the two parted ways, with Barnabas taking his cousin Mark with him. Years later Mark must have repented for his attitude and Paul welcomed him back in Rome as an accepted companion and co-worker (see Col. 4:10; Philemon 24). During Paul's imprisonment in Rome, he sought John Mark's presence as a useful co-worker.

What Do We Learn from These Conflict Stories in the Bible?

In the first story of Cain and Abel, the conflict was not resolved, and the story ended in murder. The two stories that followed in the New Testament were resolved and ended in reconciliation. We may not be able to totally avoid conflicts in ministry or families or life in general, but we *must,* as Christ followers, be willing to resolve them at all costs or we will suffer the consequences of these broken relationships. And most importantly, it hurts the cause of world evangelism.

One of the best examples of restored relationships is Joseph, the favorite son of Jacob, who was betrayed and abandoned by his brothers. He did have his own shortcomings in boasting about his dreams and gifts before his siblings. but he certainly didn't deserve to be dumped into a pit and sold as a slave to merchants passing by. (see Genesis 37)

The Lord God, however, blessed and prospered Joseph. When his brothers showed up in Egypt, Joseph initially had difficulty in facing his past. By the time he saw his brothers again, Joseph had been Prime Minister for nearly a decade. Joseph could travel anywhere he wanted, yet he chose not to return to Canaan. He knew where to find his family, but he chose not to contact them. Joseph was content to forget his past; however, God was focused on a future reconciliation. (see Genesis 41)

People from all the surrounding countries came to Joseph in Egypt to buy grain because the famine was so severe (see Genesis 41:57). And Joseph's brothers were also experiencing the drastic effects of the famine and eventually had to go to Egypt for grain. The brothers didn't recognize him. His beard was shaved, his robe was royal, and the language he spoke was Egyptian. It never occurred to them that they were standing before their baby brother!

Thinking the prince couldn't understand Hebrew, the brothers spoke to him by pointing to what they wanted and speaking with their eyes and gestures. Joseph called for a Hebrew-speaking servant to translate. Then Joseph admonished his brothers acting like a stranger and spoke roughly to them. The brothers fell face-first in the dirt which then brought to Joseph's mind "the childhood dream" (see Genesis 42:7).

Joseph asked about their family. Joseph's brothers' response was that the youngest was now with their father, and that one of them was no longer living (see Genesis 42:13). This was the first time he had heard anything from his family in twenty years! Jacob was alive. Benjamin was alive. And it must have deeply affected Joseph when they said, "and one is no more." The brothers assumed Joseph was probably dead.

This was the toughest challenge of Joseph's life. Suppose Joseph had refused his brothers and gotten vengeance by dismissing them and letting them suffer through the famine? What if he washed his hands of the whole mess? God's plan for the nation of Israel depended upon the compassion of Joseph. A lot was at stake here.

There is a lot at stake with us, too. Yes, our history might have some sad chapters. You can break the cycle of broken relationships that extend for many years—even when they affect the next generation of children who take up a parent's offenses. You don't have to pass on a legacy of pain and mistrust and the sinful attitudes that come with it.

Family pain is the deepest of all pains because it oftentimes is experienced at very young ages involving people who should have been trustworthy. God transforms us by changing the way we think. (see Romans 12:2.

God will replace childish immature thinking patterns with truth. (see 1 Corinthians 13:11) You are God's child and his special creation. You are destined for heaven as part of his eternal family if you believe Jesus died for your sins and was raised from the dead.

God wants to set us on the path to reconciliation. Joseph's path of reconciliation took many years. He experienced great trials and struggles, but kept his faith in God. After three days, Joseph took the first step toward reconciliation and released his brothers from jail. He played the tough guy again: "Go on back. But I want to see this kid brother you talk about. I'll keep one of you as a guarantee." (see Genesis 42:19–20)

> Then they said to one another, "We are truly guilty concerning our brother, for we saw the anguish of his soul when he pleaded with us, and we would not hear; therefore, this distress has come upon us" (Genesis 42:21 NKJV).

We know the end of the story with the famous text in the Bible after he was reconciled with his brothers.

> But Joseph said to them, "Don't be afraid. Am I in the place of God? You intended to harm me, but God intended it for good to accomplish what is now being done, the saving of many lives. So then, don't be afraid. I will provide for you and your children." And he reassured them and spoke kindly to them (Gen. 50:19–21 NIV).

Do you remember why his brothers sold him into slavery in the first place? The short answer is found in Genesis 37:8 and 19. "They hated him all the more because of his dream." They mockingly called Joseph 'that dreamer.' Your dream will inspire more people, no doubt. But your dream will also summon more opposition. Why? Because you are disrupting the status quo. Your dream will cause a wide variety of reactions, including jealousy, envy and anger. (See Genesis 37:18–19).

Can all of us be tempted to have this same attitude when we ourselves are misunderstood? Might we respond improperly when we are betrayed or slandered or our motives are judged wrongly?

I mention all these biblical examples to now give a present-day example of unresolved conflicts which led to broken relationship among dear brothers. Christian friends should be able to resolve their conflicts, but at times, the division is so great that it takes a repentant heart and the deep work of the Holy Spirit or a Christian mediator who is not part of either party to change attitudes and lives.

While writing this book, I asked Paul Miantona, the ULICAF Board Chair at that time, to give me his honest view of my performance as a leader and his understanding of the conflict that started in ULICAF.

First, he listed many positive things about my leadership of ULICAF and LICC:

1. You were a complete servant-leader: a leader that everyone looked up to, a visionary who got things done.

2. You gave your entire life to ULICAF and laid the foundation for the organization. You are one of the key people that made it possible for LICC to exist today.

3. You are gifted at fundraising, and you connected ULICAF to incredible donors.

4. Apart from God, ULICAF/LICC wouldn't have accomplished all that it did without you. You invested your time and energy to make sure ULICAF succeeded. You made your entire family excited about the vision and they were also so involved.

5. We were like one big family. Everyone admired you tremendously. You were down-to-earth and connected with everyone. More importantly, you and another leader were like brothers. You had his back, and he had your back. Your wife and his wife had a mother-daughter type of relationship.

Now to the less positive feedback. First, the official reasons:

1. The Board realized that ULICAF was not a *missionary sending* organization, and that to become a missionary sending organization, many things had to be put in place. Additionally, ULICAF was not in the position to go through all the processes involved to become a missionary sending organization. This was something that should have been looked at prior to the dedication in Minnesota.

2. The Board was also not prepared nor had the financial strength to cover the salary costs for both the outgoing Executive Director and the incoming Executive Director at the same time. For these reasons, the board, in faith, made an offer that they thought could have been manageable for the organization. The offer, however, was rejected.

I asked Paul to go a little bit deeper. I asked him if there were additional accusations that the Board members had against me either officially or as rumors.

He noted, as I had known, that the Board was divided in its opinions:

"One group felt that, despite the many great things that you did for the organization, you did something that the Board disagreed with."

His response hit me very deeply. This disagreement was with someone close to me. To protect the privacy of all involved, I will not give this person's name. This situation between another leader and me led to conflict in the organization.

Paul went on to say:

"One of the main things that led to the conflict was that, in my opinion, you and he were not willing to work out your differences. The two of you, who were our key leaders, were completely divided. As a Board President, I could see this, and I still do see a huge division between you. The relationship that existed was thrown out of the window. This I am afraid could bring a lasting division among both families, especially, your children. Every time I talked to the either of you, you were very diplomatic, but not as honest as necessary about what was going on. I still feel terribly disappointed about how things have become between you, as well as your families. I am afraid that things might never, ever be the same again."

He continued:

"Dr. Buor, to be frank, I sit and feel very sad to see how things have become. Growing up, you have been one of the leaders that I have always admired, and I still do admire you. You stood out among other Inland leaders. You connected with the Inlanders here in the States, as well as in Liberia very well. What you have done by leading the construction of LICC will forever be remembered. I wish we had remained together. It is my prayer that there will someday be an honest and sincere reconciliation. However, that reconciliation needs to start with you and (the other leader), as well as your families.

Like you, I am going through leadership struggles. Several of us have not communicated for almost a year now, and I feel terribly sad. As a leader here, I want to finish well. Starting is easy, but finishing is very difficult. I hope that someday we can collaborate (you and ULICAF). There are many things that we could do together. For instance, students from your college preparatory high school (RICA) could be given scholarships to attend LICC. Your school could be a feeder school to LICC. Also, education (teacher training) students who are in their last year at LICC, could do internships at your school (RICA). You could also provide jobs for LICC graduates.

I pray and hope that we can all come together and have a reconciliatory celebration. There is nothing impossible with God."

So, I do have opportunities before me for reconciliation by doing my part and being open as a result of these admonitions. In heaven, all the human frailties will disappear. I know we will be reconciled brothers then. But, my hope and prayer for everyone that experiences conflict is, if it is possible, that reconciliation will happen here on earth. Let's do ourselves and the church a good favor. Please be open to God's work in this area of your life.

There is a lesson here for new visionary leaders. Look at an example from David's unfulfilled desire to build a temple for God. Because David was a warrior, God wanted Solomon, David's son, to build the temple. The Lord did, however, give David the construction plans which he passed on to Solomon his son (see I Chronicles 28:10–12).

God opens and closes doors, arranges circumstances, and sometimes creates a trajectory that you didn't expect. The story of David illustrates how it is possible to achieve your dream after you are dead that could not be achieved directly by you while alive. We can learn the importance of dreaming beyond our lifetime. I pray that LICC will in some way have the same impact on some future generation of leaders who will be trained to spread the gospel across Liberia and beyond.

Let me summarize the chapter with great insight I have learned. Dr. Mensa Otabil is one of my most admired preachers from Ghana, West Africa. On February 2, 2020, he delivered a stunning message, "Learning Excellence through Pressure." In Exodus 27:20, while Israel was still living in the wilderness, God commanded them to bring pure oil from pressed olives for the lighted candles so that the lamps could continually burn in the Tabernacle.

Here are four specific instructions:

1. Use **a tiny olive** fruit about 3 centimeters for oil.
2. Next **press or beat the fruit**, a process by which the fruit breaks open and produces oil.
3. **Pure oil** will eventually be a high quality due to the filtration process of the constant beating, pressing, and squeezing.
4. **The pure oil is then used to light the tabernacle. It will be a beautifully clear light** that *does not produce smoke and repel people.*

Here is a spiritual application in those specific instructions.

- When God wants to take you to the next level of your spiritual life, He will bring you through trials and struggles (breaking open your fruit through the pressures of life).
- Light is the benefit (blessing) that the squeezing process creates. It shines Christ to other people.

- God loves us with His benevolence, but is not satisfied with our character until we "ooze out" the precious fruit of the Spirit.
- God not only loves, but carefully prepares the people He uses.

So, do not be dismayed when God begins the pounding, squeezing and filtration process in you. Instead, know that your next level assignment is on the way. For me, the journey I am currently on has been incredible, and by far the most joyous chapter of my life. I have experienced God's presence and His power and that experience has come in my weakness.

Chapter 15: The Story of LICC Continues

I will always appreciate my role as the founding President of LICC. However, I was always open to the possibility that one day I would be passing on the baton of leadership to somebody else once we saw our dreams for LICC come to fruition.

LICC currently offers only associate degrees while the long-term dream of a 4-year college or university is still in development. The school does offer degrees in education, theology, business management, and agriculture.

The long-term plan includes other degrees such as nursing, engineering, leadership, and law.

Here is a snapshot of how LICC is doing. In February 2020, I had the opportunity to sit down with President Nuwoe-James Kiamu, the current President of LICC, and I asked him how the school was progressing. He gave me a very honest evaluation of the school.

Let me first explain how the president initially got connected to LICC. He became President at the request of Mr. Dehpue Zuo, the Liberian board chairman, who diligently pursued the emergency help of Nuwoe-James Kiamu. LICC had been without a president for some time and was facing closure. According to the Ministry of National Commission on Higher Education's (NCHE) guidelines, no college or university can function legally in Liberia without a qualified president with an earned Ph.D. or a doctorate from an accredited academic institution. So, the board chair set out to find a new president and found Dr. Kiamu.

Prior to accepting the position at LICC, Dr. Kiamu was a part-time lecturer at the Liberia Baptist Theological Seminary and also the director of his own graduate school, the Evangelical Theological

Seminary of Liberia (ETSEL). Further, Dr. Kiamu was seriously contemplating joining a political party and hoped to become a vice-presidential candidate. Unfortunately, Dr. Kiamu had to temporarily put his position at Liberia Baptist Theological Seminary on hold. This also delayed his securing NCHE accreditation for ETSEL from the higher education ministry for that school. So, after several appeals by the LICC board, on October 11, 2016, he accepted their request to serve as the school's president for just one semester. As interim President of LICC, he was responsible to help search for a permanent president with the goal of stabilizing the institution.

At the end of the semester, Dr. Kiamu accomplished the two tasks he agreed to and reported this to the board. However, the board at that time did not have the financial resources to hire a qualified president. The board chair, again, asked for a grace period—another semester. With a graceful spirit, Dr. Kiamu continues to lead the school without knowing when he will be relieved by a permanent President.

From an Interview with Dr. Nuwoe-James Kiamu, President of LICC, February 12, 2020

So, how is the school doing? The school is doing well, and not so well. It is doing well because its doors are still open, and LICC is still graduating students, though at a much smaller number than what we had hoped. The fact that students still are being educated there and receiving degrees is the good news!

On the other hand, the school is not doing well because of numerous challenges and obstacles. The first one is the continuing and endless financial struggles. The government that once provided substantial funds to subsidize LICC has ceased. Starting in 2010, the national government under the leadership of President Ellen Johnson-Sirleaf allotted $100,000 annually to LICC's development. Similarly, the county government allotted $20,000 annually to subsidize disadvantaged students. Both subsidies have now ceased.

ULICAF, the founding organization of LICC, is unable to provide any substantial assistance. This is because the influence of the United Liberia Inland Church Associates and Friends (ULICAF) in the United States has diminished, so its fundraising capability has decreased. From its inception in 2003, ULICAF had served as the strongest support-raising arm for LICC. ULICAF's funding helped purchase the 24.5 acres of land of the current campus and funded the academic building, the library building, the faculty guesthouse, and the agricultural research center.

Unfortunately, most of our American friends and partners, those who started with us in the beginning, have retired, died, or are no longer donors. Some of our partner churches have taken on new passions and new partners in different parts of the world.

Thirdly, due to a continuing economic downturn in Liberia, students are finding it extremely difficult to pay their school fees. The unemployment rate is still very high with no end in sight.

Fourthly, just like in America, Liberia is struggling with COVID-19 and was locked-down from the beginning. At the beginning of the pandemic, you could not cross the county or country borders—even to purchase any needed goods. Although restrictions have lessened since then, Liberia is still recovering from COVID's impact on the economy. There were very few new businesses started and many businesses shut down, obviously causing unemployment to skyrocket.

The agricultural program that was envisioned as a source of additional income has not paid off. Its products are still at the experimental level and apparently the agricultural program has currently lost its original vision to teach Liberians new farming techniques as well as raise money for LICC.

But in light of these predicaments and despite all of these challenges, Dr. Kiamu is determined to vigorously pursue the mission and vision of the institution. That is good news! He has challenged his staff and faculty to pursue:

- **Godliness:** remaining a Christ-centered learning environment, and providing students with knowledge of God and His creation.

- **Excellence:** excelling and moving beyond all mediocrities.

- **Accountability:** producing leaders who are accountable for their own lives and possessions, and contributing to nation-building.

- **Resourcefulness:** having resources and not being resourceful is the beginning of poverty and the miseries. LICC is determined to train and graduate more resourceful (rather that reckless) leaders.

- **Stewardship:** serving, managing something or someone's property. LICC is determined to train leaders who will serve their God, families, and nation well, instead of demanding to be served.

Also, a new faculty member has been hired to initiate the process of launching a nursing program soon.

Finally, Dr. Kiamu is determined to carry out and implement the strategic plan that was developed four years ago. That plan involves the construction of additional infrastructure on the campus when LICC's financial situation improves, hopefully, in the near future. Also, he is actively working with the Ministry of the National Commission for Higher Education to receive certification for bachelor's degrees.

LICC was planted by the United Liberia Inland Church (the legal owner of LICC) as a university with the help of ULICAF back in the United States. LICC was built, brick-by-brick, with the vision to help redevelop and rebuild Liberia through education to develop leaders in every area of Liberian society. That has not changed. During my season as its leader, we pursued that dream. My prayers are with Dr. Kiamu as he leads LICC into the future.

I will discuss in more detail in another chapter the legal ownership of LICC and why the specific structure of LICC is important for its long-term success.

My Path to Continued Involvement with LICC

First, I will always pray for LICC, its staff and students. Wherever I travel, I will tell the amazing story of LICC and share the school's

131

needs with our friends and those who might become our friends. One of the pressing needs of LICC is the development of partnerships with individuals, churches, and academic institutions. I invite and encourage all LICC's founding members, specifically Liberians, to support the institution. I now see myself as a pro-bono advocate for helping to develop more partners for the school. Currently, the school of agriculture is benefiting from such a partnership. Several years ago, my friend Donald Cassell introduced me to Gina and her husband from Frankfurt, Indiana. The couple had planned to serve in East Africa. But the specific country in which they had planned to live was at war. So, I met with the couple and convinced them to come with me to Liberia, and they did. We signed a five-year memorandum of understanding to serve in our agriculture department. They faithfully served at LICC, and when the five years was over, they asked other friends of theirs to replace them.

The departments of education, business, and theology would greatly benefit from international partnerships as well.

For long term survival, the school needs to develop projects that support the school. Dr. Kiamu shared with me that the United Liberia Inland Church (ULIC) has donated fifty acres of land to the school. The school can use the land to plant cash crops such as cocoa, rubber trees, and palm. Within three to five years these cash crops could generate a considerable income for LICC. One of the institutions that is benefiting from cash crops in Liberia is Cuttington University which gets an annual return of about one million United States dollars from its rubber farm. Although it might not produce as much revenue as Cuttington University's farm, I am hopeful that LICC will pattern itself after this school to develop the land to generate similar sources of income.

Further Good News

Shortly after I was writing this section, in August 2020, I received the following email from LICC President Nuwoe:

Subject: LICC'S Elevation

Greetings Dr. and Mrs. Buor,

I pray that this communication finds you in great health.

I write to first thank God and then you both, for the pioneering work you did to establish LICC.

By God's grace, the NCHE has finally elevated the school to a bachelor's degree granting status. The NCHE Board of Commissioners on 14th August 2020, informed me in a letter from its Secretariat of the Commissioners' decision to elevate LICC. Together with LICC's Owners, LICC Board of Trustees, Faculty, Staff and Student Body, I am pleased to say a huge "thank God" for the development, and a large "thank you" to you and your family.

The seed you sowed has grown and is beginning to blossom. By God's grace, it will tower to become what you envisaged.

May the Lord strengthen you as He does LICC. Please accept my deep appreciations as we continue to serve together to make this dream outlive us.

Have a blessed week.

Growing in His Likeness,

Nuwoe-James Kiamu

In the New Testament, Jesus calls his disciples to look beyond their own aspirations and grasp the greatness of their calling. He specifically asks the disciples to look beyond their mediocre ambition and embrace who God has made them to be:

> "You are the light of the world. A city set on a hill cannot be hidden. Neither do people light a lamp and put it under a bowl. Instead, they put it on its stand, and it gives light to everyone in the house. In the same way, let your light shine before others, that they may see your good deeds and glorify your Father in heaven" (Matthew 5:14–16 NIV).

Class of 2021 Commencement

In October 2021, I received a letter from President Kiamu and his program committee asking me to serve as the guest speaker at the college's 7th graduation. I was thrilled to put everything aside and to serve the college in this way. And on December 11, 2021, I served as the guest speaker at Liberia International College's first Bachelor's degree commencement ceremony.

My speech was titled *Pursue a Path of Meaningful Life.* I encouraged the students to set a guidepost (North Star) in their lives of Faith, Hope, and Love based on I Corinthians 13:13.

> Three things will last forever—faith, hope, and love—and the greatest of these is love (1 Cor. 13:13 NLT).

Faith is the foundation you always turn to in the midst of anything—even when the sea rises and fills your boat and it's about to sink.

Hope is what keeps us moving. Staying hopeful is what will propel you forward on the days that you don't want to move any longer.

Finally, love is the greatest gift of all. The very message that I heard from God when I became a Christian was about His love for me and the whole world. We were all made to love others, and I've found that we live our best lives and we are at our most successful when loving others is our ultimate focus.

Even though I am no longer involved with LICC on a daily basis, I love those students. They represent part of Liberia's future. Yet, there is something even more important than my love. The most important thing is that they know that God loves each and every one of them.

Part 5

My Ongoing Education

Chapter 16: What I Have Learned – Preparing for the Transition

With age comes experience and with experience comes wisdom. The story of RICA and CLTI is just beginning. Valuable lessons I learned from my experience leading ULICAF and founding LICC will help me in decision-making with RICA. Yet, for all the good that is coming from that experience, the start of CLTI began with a conflict in ULICAF's leadership that was both surprising and unwanted.

We accomplished many projects the right way. From the very beginning of Liberia International Christian College, we clearly established that the United Liberia Inland Church would be the legal owner of LICC. The land deeds and all other legal documents were processed in the name of United Liberia Inland Church (ULIC), our primary partner in Liberia. ULIC has a long history in Liberia, dating back to 1938, and the church continues to grow nationally. In 1978, during my high school years, I surrendered my life to Jesus Christ through the ministry of a ULIC evangelist. I was nurtured, mentored, and grown in their leadership circle at a national level.

Unfortunately, the cooperation between the Buor family and ULICAF broke down as there was a communication misunderstanding which developed into an open ongoing conflict. Since that time the tensions have been ongoing, sometimes quietly and sometimes with heated emotion.

Older members have lamented the loss of the dynamic, active ULICAF fellowship that they helped to build and maintain over several years. I think the truth is that no one can explain the complexity of the sort of confusion that occurred. As the apostle Paul says,

Now we see things imperfectly, like puzzling reflections in a mirror, but then we will see everything with perfect clarity. All that I know now is partial and incomplete, but then I will know everything completely, just as God now knows me completely. Three things will last forever—faith, hope, and love—and the greatest of these is love (1 Cor. 13:12–13 NLT).

But our hope and prayers are that despite our differences we will forgive one another and walk in love knowing that Jesus has forgiven us our sins and so we must forgive one another.

In 2013, during my visit to Liberia, we invited former leaders including the President, all regional leaders, and those in the current administration, to review the legal documents for LICC. The newly established ownership of LICC helped ease the transition and avoided some of the problems that happened to ULICAF in America in 2014.

We had very promising beginnings. From its establishment in 2000 up until 2014, ULICAF grew numerically and had a definite spiritual influence among the Liberian refugees in the United States. ULICAF's mission to rebuild war-torn Liberia was a major concern for them and opened doors to be able to support projects all over Liberia. Those were exciting times as God brought many volunteers to assist us in several philanthropy projects.

For 10 years we had annual conferences which helped to build relationships and raise thousands of dollars for projects such as building a guest house in Liberia, supporting several churches, and building LICC. We also established sponsorships for orphans and underprivileged youth to pursue nursing skills at various universities through our ministry *One Hour for Christ*.

In 2014, we held our annual conference in Minnesota. This conference was the first time we established a transition in the leadership. My wife and I were commissioned to return to Liberia to work with LICC, and a new leader was chosen to take my place as the Executive Director for the US office of ULICAF here in America. It was an exciting and joyous time of new beginnings.

Within just two weeks after the celebration, our vibrant, tight-knit organization sadly began to quickly break apart! We did try to heal the misunderstandings—albeit, without success.

What was the most important lesson I learned? I didn't realize at the time how vital it was to adequately prepare for this transition. "What did I do wrong?" I thought. I started studying other examples of leadership transition. They emphasized that the leader is the one that sets the tone for the ongoing of the whole organization. The following are two stories about *best practices* in preparing for transition.

Grace Church in Noblesville, Indiana, prepared for many years when they anticipated a planned transition in Senior Pastors. Our family attended Grace church from 2002 to 2015, and Yah also served Grace Church as a custodian for almost 12 years.

Dave Rodriguez was the founding and Senior Pastor of Grace Church. Grace Church was the daughter of Faith Church (91st Street and College Ave. in Indianapolis, IN) and had financial support from Faith for five years. Dave had been the Youth Pastor at Faith and was commissioned as the Pastor of Grace and between half and three-fourths of Faith's congregation left to start Grace. It was a process that was thought through and put into place after a failed attempt to start a daughter church. The group that was to become Grace Church met regularly to put together their documents and to talk through how they planned to staff childcare, have a youth group, etc. over a period of two years before the church was actually launched.

Grace started in a warehouse in 1994 and by 2010, the Church grew to almost 8,000 members. Grace is very active in the community and has planted six more churches in the United States plus several other churches internationally. It also has a very extensive benevolence food pantry and care ministry and does various outreaches to internationals as well as supporting a number of missionaries.

In 2011, Dave announced his plans for retirement. Following Dave's announcement, the governing board created a roadmap for a five-year succession plan. They started with focused times of prayer followed by a tedious search for a new senior pastor. This was followed by countless meetings and extensive interviews of potential candidates.

In the third year, they decided on Barry Rodriguez, Dave's son, as a *potential* candidate. Eventually, he was selected as the best choice. Barry was given the opportunity to learn different aspects of church leadership while Dave remained by his side for another two years. Finally, after another vote of the members, Barry was confirmed as the new Senior Pastor and Dave turned over the leadership role to him.

This transition process, though slow and methodical, seems to have worked well. Today, Grace is continuing its work, although there has been transition obstacles with some members leaving and the leadership adjusting to financial challenges and obvious COVID-19 problems.

Now, let's look at another partner church we know quite well. Northwest Covenant Church (NWCC) is in Mount Prospect, Illinois. In 1997, our family moved to Mount Prospect, and became part of NWCC from that time until 2001 while I was working on my doctoral studies at Loyola University.

Pastor Paul Thompson, the senior pastor, eventually took another call to lead another Covenant Church in Arizona. And thus, the search for a new senior pastor began. A pastor search committee was set up and after two long years the committee finally recommended a potential candidate, and he became the new pastor.

The Church is thriving today and continues to grow as they stand on the strong foundation of God's Word. A few years ago, I met with a member of the congregation and asked him, "Why did they take so long to hire a new pastor?"

This parishioner told me that when a pastor departs, there is a tendency for individuals to have strong opinions on the best type of person to be the senior pastors' replacement (personality, teaching style, age, etc.) to lead the future direction of the church's ministry. He said if the pastoral search committee had moved too quickly with their succession plan, there was bound to be conflict.

What are the lessons learned from these two examples?

First, prayer is essential and is where to begin. Let's look at Nehemiah's life as a good example of leadership principles. Nehemiah said,

> For some days I mourned and fasted and prayed before the God of heaven... Lord, let your ear be attentive to the prayer of this your servant and to the prayer of your servants who delight in revering your name. Give your servant success today by granting him favor in the presence of this man (Nehemiah 1:4, 11 NKJV).

Like Nehemiah, the amount of time we spend in prayer can indicate whether we are really trusting in God or in our own natural ability and wisdom to make things happen.

Second, Grace Church and Northwest Covenant Church both took time to pray and search carefully to find the right person for their leadership continuity and for the spiritual growth of their congregations.

Unlike these two church examples, the ULICAF leadership transition process occurred in just a few months. The result was conflict and broken relationships which obviously led to the hindrance of carrying on the original vision and mission of the school.

We failed to pray and allow enough time for our succession plan to succeed. We also failed to search broadly for the right person to lead us into the future we had envisioned. As a result, this once-thriving organization, that was embraced and strongly supported by both Liberians and Americans, fell into conflict, and eventually into chaos and disintegration.

So, what I am doing differently as the founder Christian of Leadership Training International? From the earliest stages of the development of CLTI I have involved one of my daughters in CLTI's leadership. If something happens to me physically or, preferably, some years ahead when I retire, we can trust God for effective leadership continuity in our organization. Currently, Tonzia is serving on CLTI's board as the Chief Communications Officer. She gives generously of her time, finances and skills. She is a Vice President of Human Resources of a major hospital in Nashville, Tennessee.

Chapter 17: What I Have Learned – It's About More than Finding the Right People

A team is more than the strengths and talents of its individual players. It is important how the players work together and support each other. In his book *The 17 Indisputable Laws of Teamwork: Embrace and Empower Your Team* famous author John Maxwell (p. 77) identified three kinds of team players when a game is on the line:

1. *Players who don't want the ball*: This player may not have the ability to come through for the team during high-pressure situations. Typically, they play to their strengths and understand their limitations. They are the backbone of the team.

2. *Players who want the ball but shouldn't have it.* This second type is not the winner that is needed, and typically cannot carry the team to victory when the game is on the line. They do not understand their limitations and their egos are greater than their strengths. Although they may enjoy individual success, they can be dangerous to the team.

3. *Players who want the ball and should have it.* This is usually the smallest group in your team, but they are the deliverers. They have the ability to carry the team to the next level even when the going gets tough! For an example of this type of player think of the famous basketball players Michael Jordan of the Chicago Bulls or Reggie Miller of the Pacers. They were capable of coming through when the pressure was on.

Big goals require a team. That is why President Lyndon Johnson said, "There are no problems we cannot solve together, and very few that we can solve by ourselves." (Maxwell, page 4)

Our previous organization, ULICAF, had a team, most of whom had no previous experience serving on the board of a non-profit. We did some amazing things and had great potential for growth even without this board experience.

Unfortunately, though, some players did not grow in wisdom to lead a non-profit ministry or develop their leadership skills. Some did not understand their specific role on the board. As a result, the road to our next major goal was always an uphill battle with the continual danger of sliding backwards. Sometimes the team lost focus which led to decreased energy and a breakdown in unity that resulted in a loss in momentum. We failed to reach "championship" caliber.

To be successful, we needed to focus on our work in Liberia and work in unity. Instead, some members of our leadership team were manipulated by someone who had lost sight of the big picture. Instead of Liberia, everything revolved around their needs, their goals, and their desires. This self-focus did not bode well for ULICAF.

After ULICAF's feud, when it became time to recruit a new board for CLTI, I made the recruiting process very selective. First, I focused on the first "Who" principle in Jim Collins' book which states, "do whatever you can to get the right people on the bus, the wrong people off the bus, and the right people into the right seats."

Jim Collins asserts that greatness flows first and foremost from having the right people in the key seats. (*Good to Great: Why Some Companies Make the Leap...And Others Don't,* p. 14)

First, I started with a very small team, three persons whom I have known for a long time and valued their trust and input.

Second, I challenged myself to start focusing on moving forward with our new vision and journey and forgetting the distractions of the past conflicts.

Now that time has elapsed and more healing has been taking place on both sides, we are seeing an opportunity for some Liberians to become ministry partners. As we plan to return to the States when the COVID-19 travel restriction is lifted, we hope to visit some of our long-time Liberian friends who are already supporting the current work with CLTI.

Part 6

Messages to Supporters

Chapter 18: My Message to Those Who Stayed

Thanks! Because of you, CLTI is moving forward at a rapid pace! May God continue to bless you. CLTI's mission is training the next generation of leaders for Liberia. We are working to develop leaders who will serve Christ regardless of culture. From its start in 2015, God has blessed CLTI with an incredible team, both in United States and in Liberia.

There is a saying that "one is too small to achieve greatness." A Chinese proverb states, "Behind an able man there are always other able men" (or able men and women).

Behind CLTI is a dedicated team that I regard as my personal heroes. When Yah and I felt God's call to continue in His Kingdom work in Liberia, He gave us a clear and big vision. I quickly turned to two dear friends to brainstorm at a coffee table. I consider this our first team meeting, and we established the name: *Christian Leadership Training International (CLTI).*

A second meeting was scheduled. A board of directors was identified and contacted. The process of establishing a new non-profit ministry was begun!

From that small beginning, our team has expanded numerically to include a board of directors, a customer service coordinator, a web manager and newsletter editor, a chief communications officer, and a networking coordinator. In Liberia, God has gifted CLTI with a vibrant, dedicated, and God-fearing team that includes an entrepreneurship manager, a discipleship leader, an engineer, a project manager, security, and a host of daily workers.

CLTI is a winning team because it has winning players who make things happen. For example, when CLTI needed a website developed, Louise and Tonzia developed it. When CLTI needed $20,000 to purchase a property for a new campus, the team players made it happen. Our players are still making things happen, doing whatever it takes to push our cause to the next level. So, we are becoming confident, elevated, and amazed by what God is doing.

Ultimately, CLTI embarked on developing a college preparatory high school facility in the city of Gompa, Liberia, at an estimated cost of half a million dollars. The new school, Riverview International Christian Academy is off and running. On November 1, 2021, RICA officially opened and enrolled 440 students from grades 1 through 11. Also, because of CLTI's support, I was able to hire 30 instructional staff and 20 support staff ranging from security to custodians and grounds workers. And on November 12, RICA was dedicated. But we are just getting started. Immediately following the dedication, CLTI broke ground for a state-of-the-art cafeteria (building designed by Ewers' Architectural firm in Colorado). The cafeteria will serve as the feeding center, as a campus church/chapel for more than 600 students and 50 instructional and support staff, and as a community gathering space. God is already using you, our partners, to plan and provide quality Christian education and multiply the reach of the gospel seed. We are excited for you to see this for yourselves when you visit RICA and Liberia.

Our goal is to continually pray and invite the right team players to work with CLTI and to serve Christ, to promote unity among them, and assemble the needed resources to help reach our goal.

Chapter 19: My Message to Those Who Left and Are Returning

Thank you for your help!

I like to think that when the church grew by leaps and bounds at Pentecost, that most, if not all, of the 70 disciples returned (see Luke 10:1–24).

Take the First Step

In September 2019, I received a phone call while running errands in Monrovia, Liberia. Although it had been more than five years, I recognized the voice and became suspicious. The caller gave his name and quickly went into explaining the reason for his call. He admitted that he had called to apologize. He further explained that for several years he had said all manner of things about me that were not true. He had called because he wanted my forgiveness. I let him know I was driving and concerned about using the phone at the same time. I asked if we could have the conversation at another time.

About a week or two later, he called again. It was the same thing: he was asking for forgiveness. I thanked him but said it had been seven or more years since we had been in association. I also felt led to ask him if he could tell me anything that I did wrong that triggered him to go about tarnishing my reputation. He explained that when he and his wife shared their vision with me, I had not embraced their vision and they had felt hurt.

Grant Forgiveness

Then I remembered what he was talking about. Very early in our ministry, he was one of our promising leaders. However, he had decided to form his own ministry with a different focus. My wife and I prayed with them, gave them our blessing, and sent them on their way. God does not lead everyone down the same path; we had wished him well on his journey, but that didn't mean we were going to change the focus of our ministry. Finally, I told him I understood how it seemed from his perspective. I prayed with him, and we both forgave one another.

Several others who initially walked with us in the beginning stages of our ministry later were offended over some aspect of our ministry and left us. Some have called us or visited us directly to reconcile with us. We have shared a meal together and prayed. Some of these friends are now supporting our current ministry financially on a regular basis while others continue to encourage and pray for us regularly.

Give Grace

While I was writing this chapter, I had an encounter. We were behind schedule in getting a piece of the construction job done for the school. So, I called a friend in Monrovia, and he sent me five young men to help.

There were two carpenters, two masons, and a steel bender. When they arrived, we discussed their compensations and they all felt the financial arrangements were satisfactory. Just two days into the work, the team leader suddenly expressed dissatisfaction with the compensation and took his group and went back to Monrovia. Although we would have preferred they stayed and worked for the agreed upon wage, we let them out of the contract.

A day after their departure, I received a call from the steel bender asking if he could come back to Ganta to continue his job. He explained that it was the team leader that manipulated the team to leave the work, thinking he would get me to increase their pay. The steel bender, however, said that he was satisfied with his contract agreement, and he would like to return and work. I accepted his appeal, and the steel bender joined us in Ganta, doing a beautiful job.

Have No Regrets

I share this story for a reason. Sometimes we are manipulated by the plans of others and a decision is made that we come to regret. The steel bender was blessed with work and will likely receive more work in the future. The others missed out on a great opportunity to help finish a school that will bless the children of Liberia. I hope you do not let the motivation and influence of others keep you from God's calling and blessings in your life.

Chapter 20: My Message to Those Who Left

I am not striking back or condemning anyone. Thanks for what you did do. Thanks for helping us provide education for Liberian children and adults.

We still care and we hope that one day, if that is God's plan, you will tread this path with us again. And if we were at fault—even in a small way—I ask for forgiveness.

I pray that God will be able to restore our broken relationships—if not on this earth, then it will happen in heaven. So, I wish all of you friends who left, that you go on serving our Savior! Hopefully, wherever you are, in whatever you are doing, you are dedicating your efforts to Him. If you trust God and dedicate your work to Him, He will bless it. That is the same prayer I pray for myself.

One day, when we meet in heaven, it will all be clearer. The stubborn frailties of human ego will have dropped away, and we will worship Him as one. We will remember fondly the good He allowed us to do together on earth. Then, finally, we will be together in Christ forever.

Part 7

Leadership Principles

Chapter 21: Leadership Lessons I Have Learned and Now Share with You

Those who have known me a long time know that my journey as a Christian leader has been a long one. And it has had its ups and downs. It was a great joy knowing my mother and many others in our village gave their lives to Christ. A great sadness is not knowing whether I will see my earthly father in heaven. I have taught in schools and pastored or co-pastored at churches in Liberia, the Gambia, and Nairobi, Kenya. I have seen my country racked by civil war and been a refugee. I was able to return to Liberia to found what is considered by many to be the first college in West Africa founded by Africans. I, unfortunately, had to part ways with that organization. As you know as a reader of this book, I am now leading the effort to build the first college preparatory high school in Gompa, Nimba County, northeastern Liberia.

From those years of ministry, I have gained some wisdom. I would now like to share some of that with you. I hope my message will be helpful to all leaders (or future leaders). It is particularly focused to those who find that their path (one they felt was ordained by God to follow) has turned into a dead end.

Leaders make commitments that define how their leadership will be effective. Such commitments aren't standards that other people set for them; they are non-negotiable. A few years ago, I stopped organizing my life in terms of goals. Instead, I made personal *commitments*. These commitments help me stay focused on my mission and vision.

As a Christian leader, you are to be an influencer for Christ, an ambassador for the Lord, and a change-agent for the gospel of God.

I am sharing leadership lessons that I have learned to help you develop a list of your own commitments for your life's mission. If you let them, these lessons will become a source of great strength and guidance in your ministry. In the rest of this section, I will discuss what I consider are key lessons:

- Leadership Lesson #1: *Live* with a pursuit of God.

- Leadership Lesson #2: *Begin* with a compelling vision.

- Leadership Lesson #3: *Maintain* integrity in finances.

- Leadership Lesson #4: *Know* that some people will depart.

- Leadership Lesson #5: *Forgive* those who hurt you.

- Leadership Lesson #6: *Be strong* and *courageous.*

- Leadership Lesson #7: *Draw power* from Christ-like partners.

- Leadership Lesson #8: *Anchor* in your convictions.

- Leadership Lesson #9: *Befriend* wise people and become wise.

- Leadership Lesson #10: *Be confident,* but flexible and practical.

- Leadership Lesson #11: *Look* to God for what is next for you when the bottom falls out.

- Leadership Lesson #12: *Finish* the task.

Leadership Lesson #1: Live with a Pursuit of God

I gave my life to Jesus.

In my final year of high school in 1980, I had the privilege to believe in God and surrender my life to Jesus Christ. As a leader, my loyalty is to Jesus Christ. I choose to commit my gifts in service to Him and through that commitment to bless the world.

162

This is what we are created for: To love God with all our hearts, with all our souls, and with all our minds, and with all our strength. (see Mark 12:30)

In Acts 16:30–34, Luke records the life-transformation of a military leader (the jailer) that came to the Apostle Paul and Silas who were at that time in prison for their faith. He asked how he could be reconciled with God. Paul's straightforward answer was: "Believe in the Lord Jesus Christ, and you will be saved." The soldier immediately believed and was saved.

This story fascinates me and never grows old. I prayed as a young Liberian man and believed in Jesus Christ as my Lord and Savior. I believed that He died for my sins on the cross, rose from the dead, and promised to guide me through this life, and eventually to an eternal relationship with God.

It is an understatement to say my life would have taken an entirely different path if I had not made that choice. This is one of my motivations for working for others to know Jesus.

Leadership Lesson #2: Begin with a Compelling Vision

My vision includes my love for Liberia and my love for education.

At some point in the life of a believer, particularly one that is called to lead, God implants a vision in their minds and souls. It becomes a consuming struggle and tension of what one's life is in the present, and the character formation that God will work in your life in the future as you work out that vision. God wants you to help Him change the world, but He will also be working transformation in your life.

A leader without a vision cannot inspire people to follow him. You must develop the ability to see people, places, and things not just as

163

they are now, but how they could be in the future. The Bible says, "Where there is no vision, the people perish" (Proverbs 29:18 KJV).

The word "vision" is defined as "revelation." So, a vision is a mental picture you draw in your mind of where you now are in the *present* and what you want to accomplish or be in the *future*.

When people or a nation lack a vision or mental picture of the future, they perish. This means, practically, that things don't work out. A paraphrase from the Message puts it this way, "If people can't see what God is doing, they stumble all over themselves." (Proverbs 29:18 The Message)

Vision is foundational for all life change and progress. Until our spiritual and mental eyes see a picture of the future, we will not realize our goals in the real world. As a Christian, that vision should come from God.

A vision might begin with a concern, an issue, or some obstacle which challenges us. We might struggle with finding a solution to a pressing need. Let's look at Nehemiah for a moment.

A God-ordained vision begins as a concern. Nehemiah's vision began as a concern—a burden for his homeland and his people—not only those that were still living in Babylon, but more importantly those that had returned to Jerusalem. Nehemiah's heart was broken, which brought him to his knees; the Bible says his very countenance was changed!

Nehemiah began to pray, the best first step. A leader's prayer life is critical for vision development. A leader can't trust in his prior competence. He will eventually come to a place where he will be called to a brand-new area of skill that he has not attempted before. This is one of the ways God develops our faith and trust in Him. This is one of the ways that God gets the credit and not us.

Nehemiah prayed for two things. First, he prayed for an opportunity to bring his vision before King Artaxerxes. Nehemiah knew well that only by God's intervention would he be successful (Nehemiah 1:11 NKJV).

Second, Nehemiah prayed for compassion. Nehemiah prayed that God would move on the king's heart to provide generous financial support so that Nehemiah could fulfill his vision to rebuild the walls of Jerusalem.

> Make your servant successful today and grant him
> compassion before this man (Nehemiah 1:11b NKJV).

Nehemiah envisioned himself making the difference, not someone else, and God gave him the ability to do that. He was looking for an opportunity to work alongside God. God gives a leader vision because He trusts in the leader to find a way to step out in faith and begin the "next steps" of fulfilling the vision. A leader will also do everything practically to develop leadership skills: read books, take classes, find a mentor for advice, and start exploring various ways to get started.

New visions can die easily. When this happens part of you dies also. To avoid this, take "some" practical step forward, even if it seems small, and pray for the people that God will bring into your life to be encouragers, helpers, and financial supporters.

Back in 2015, when the Lord gave us the vision to raise up a new generation of leaders for Liberia, we invited three of our best friends to come alongside and help us develop this vision. They helped us think through a name for our organization and assisted us in steps to file for our 501(c)3. Additionally, they gave generously, and we opened our initial bank account.

Here are three questions that can help any leader clarify their vision:

1. **What breaks your heart?** When you take a deep look inside your soul (mind or heart), what breaks you? What causes you so much

discomfort that you are moved to take immediate action to find a solution? Moses wrote,

God looked down from heaven and saw the oppression of His people (Exodus 3:1 NKJV).

The suffering He saw in His people broke His heart. When I first read it, I didn't think much about it. I was wondering how I relate to that experience of the children of Israel. However, as I got older, my own heart began to break as I witnessed the suffering of the youth in Liberia. I began to understand that passage of scripture in a deep and real way.

If you watch the TV show *America's Got Talent*, you will see young people who have so much potential and talent. Some rise to the highest level and win, and some fall just short and don't win the contest. But they still have an opportunity to keep their vision going as a performer. Just being on the show is a great opportunity for them.

While growing up in Liberia, I did not have the educational opportunity that many youths have in America. But I knew that I had to make education a priority in my life to impact my country for Christ in the development of schools. I was fortunate enough to be gifted with many years of education and leadership and an overwhelming desire to inspire Liberia's youth. Because of this, I didn't look at their present predicament – devastated by years of civil war, poverty, and broken families. I saw what they "could become." I knew that they had "talent." I believed God had a vision for them, even if they didn't know it yet! Someone just needed to give them an opportunity to develop that talent. This is one of the things God uses leaders for. (see Exodus 3:7–10)

2. **What brings joy to your heart?** What makes you jump for joy and fills your heart with singing? My greatest joy is to make a real difference in people's lives. My purpose is to let God use me as His hands and feet, and for His compassion to flow through me to others in need. (see Exodus 3:10)

3. **What is your biggest dream?** If you could do anything to make the world a better place, to make a community or environmental change that would outlast you, what would you do—starting today?

Personally, I want to make a difference by educating Liberia's youth. My dream is to provide a system of innovative education to thousands of Liberians with the goal of transforming their lives, (starting at 1st grade and continuing all the way through their college years). I am offering these students an equitable access to a rigorous Christian education that prepares them to lead extraordinary lives so that they will eventually be more productive citizens of their country. I believe God has given each of us the opportunity to make a positive difference in the lives of those in our community. So, if you could accomplish anything, and knew you would succeed, what skills do you presently have that could be put to work? Again, right now?

Thus, to summarize this leadership lesson, you need to have a broken heart for some need in your community and culture, then ask yourself what would bring you great joy if the need was met. Then, finally, ask God to use the skills you have now and start taking the first steps to meeting that need.

Leadership Lesson #3: Maintain Integrity in Finances

Integrity is being honest with God, others, and yourself.

Maintain your integrity in finances and commit to be an effective steward of the resources entrusted to your care. This is an expectation of both God and man.

> *Integrity* is defined as "the practice of being honest and showing a consistent and uncompromising adherence to strong moral and ethical principles and values. In ethics, integrity is regarded as the honesty and truthfulness or accuracy of one's actions. Integrity can stand in opposition to hypocrisy, in that judging with the standards of integrity involves regarding internal consistency as a virtue and suggests that parties holding within themselves apparently conflicting values should account for the discrepancy or alter their beliefs. The word integrity evolved from the Latin adjective integer, meaning whole or complete. In this context, integrity is the inner sense of 'wholeness' deriving from qualities such as honesty and consistency of character. As such, one may judge that others have integrity to the extent that they act according to the values, beliefs and principles they claim to hold." (Taken from *The World Book Dictionary, 1969, Doubleday and Co., Inc.)*

When God calls a leader, He entrusts to him a portion of time, money/treasure, and knowledge to be invested in pursuing His first and greatest commandment—loving Him and loving our neighbor as ourselves.

> "Make every effort to be found spotless, blameless and at peace with God" (2 Peter 3:14 NIV).

By integrity, I do not claim to have it all together in every area. On the contrary, a person of integrity says, "this is where I am confident in my abilities, and this is where I am not." When you have integrity, you live out what you believe. You don't just teach truth; you model it.

For example, I don't have skill in financial management. So, there is chance I would make a serious error. Therefore, I looked for someone who is skillful and qualified in financial management. God blessed us with a woman with a degree in accounting and financial management. She is in charge and makes our reports to the IRS. She outsourced our salary payments which is most competent way to do it to make sure the right taxes are deducted and get our W2s done.

You don't need to be perfect to be an effective leader, but you do need to be transparent about your weakness. The Bible says hiding your sins leads to failure, but the one who confesses and renounces them finds mercy.

Make a commitment to be free from corruptions! Good leadership is built on trust, which stems from having a reputation for telling the truth.

A decade ago, at the early stage of our first ministry, a church exhibited a generous heart to me with a big financial gift. As I prayed about receiving the gift, I realized I did not have adequate tool in place to handle the accountability. So, I called the church treasurer and asked for the gift to be delayed until we were ready. A year later, we obtained a 501(c) 3 status and opened a bank account and identified a treasurer. Then, I called and asked for the fund to be sent to me to be used for the designated purpose.

Every gift we receive comes from the loving hand and is directed our way from God. The scripture boldly states, "Every good and perfect gift is from above, coming down from the father." (James 1:17 NIV)

In summary, leaders with integrity acknowledge their strengths as well as their weaknesses.

Do all you can now to prepare yourself for your eventual success. Your gifts will open doors, but your character will determine what you do once those doors have opened. To become a leader worth following, you must be intentional about developing your inner person. You must invest in the health of your soul. No one plans to fail, especially leaders; but to ignore the condition of your soul is equivalent to planning to fail.

Leadership Lesson #4: Know that Some People Will Depart

Not everyone will follow you the whole path that God has laid out for your life.

Jesus faced what could have been the ultimate defeat for His ministry. Yet he emerged triumphant through his relationship with his Father. His example shows us that we can do the same when faced with rejection.

John records the reaction of Jesus' disciples to His teaching in a meeting place in a town called Capernaum. He taught, "I am the Bread of life who came down out of heaven, and anyone who eats this Bread and drinks the blood will have eternal life." From that time, lots of Jesus' disciples rejected him, left, and walked with Him no more (John 6:66 NIV). Only a small nucleus of disciples remained (John 6:67 NIV).

The language indicates that the abandonment was decisive and final (see I Peter 2:6–7; I John 2:19). Jesus' response to all of this was that the supreme adversary of God operates behind failing human beings so that his malice becomes theirs.

Jesus knew the hearts of all men. He supernaturally knew that many did not believe in Him as Messiah and Son of God. They did not understand His mission; they did not understand His calling. Many of these disciples were simply attracted to the physical phenomena (e.g., miracles and food), and failed to understand the true significance of Jesus' teaching.

"If it is possible, as far as it depends on you, live at peace with everyone" (Romans 12:18 NIV). God's will is for us to live at peace with everyone, but sometimes the door to healing a broken relationship seems closed forever. A dear friend or partner can turn away in anger or, as in our case, former friends want nothing to do with us.

Why did Jesus' words cause many of His followers to desert him? Why did they walk away? We can only imagine. First, they may have realized Jesus was not going to be the conquering messiah king that they expected, Second, Jesus refused to give in to their self-centered requests. Third, Jesus emphasized faith and not deeds. Fourth, his teaching was difficult to understand and some of His words were offensive. As we grow in our faith, we may be tempted to turn away because Jesus' lessons are difficult. Will your response be to give up and ignore difficult lessons, or reject Christ?

Like with Jesus and the 70, if someone rejects us and absolutely refuses to have anything to do with us, you cannot force them to change. What we can and should do is everything we can to keep the door open to a possible reconciliation.

Jesus created the circle of twelve disciples to serve His special purposes, not the purposes of the disciples. Like the twelve, we are to serve Jesus' purposes, not those of our own invention. In the end our walk must align with God's plans.

Leadership Lesson #5: Forgive Those Who Hurt You

Remain open to forgiveness and some will return!

As a leader, I learned to forgive those who have hurt me.

You can't live in this world very long without being hurt or wounded by human bullets. Even the best of friends will disappoint you at some point. We have all been hurt. You have been hurt. I have been hurt, too. We like to think we can go about our lives unaffected by conflicts and fractures with people we care about. Unfortunately, relational breakdowns can extract energy from us and can stall our vision. The emotional impact can hang over us for as long as we draw breath.

How do we deal with this? Jesus Christ is our great example! On the cross, our Lord Jesus offered a very short prayer during excruciating hurt: He forgave those who hurt Him! Those men that Jesus forgave were government-paid killers, vicious executioners, and heartless human beings. They beat Jesus beyond recognition. Jesus hung on the cross fighting for breath and still forgave.

What kind of impact did Jesus' short prayer have on those in attendance at His crucifixion? Mark's gospel tells us that the centurion standing by said, "Truly this man was the Son of God!" (Mark 15:39 NIV)

We live in a world where so many hurt others. Let's not forget that we have hurt others, too. I am one, and you are, too. None of us is free from sin. It is human selfish nature to put ourselves first before the other person, and when we do, we hurt others.

Over the years, Jesus' short prayer of forgiveness has helped me to deal with my hurts. We are in a world filled with haters and people who will hurt us. As a Christ-follower, let your heart flow with God's daily kindness and love. (see I Cor. 13:5)

Sometimes we like to get even. If people hurt us, we might want to hurt them back, or be tempted to just end a friendship. But Jesus teaches us a different way:

> "Make every effort to live in peace with everyone and to be holy; without holiness no one will see the Lord. See to it that no one falls short of the grace of God and that no

bitter root grows up to cause trouble and defile many" (Hebrews 12:14–15 NIV).

You will be hurt in ministry, both intentionally and unintentionally. That is a guarantee! And if you are breaking new ground? Pioneers always get the arrow!

In the midst of the pain, if you allow bitterness to grow up in your life, it will choke your heart for God. It will also choke your love for people until your heart shrivels.

Spiritual leadership requires forgiveness!

Even Jesus, who was a perfect leader, was betrayed. It's not always your fault, but it will be your fault if you carry bitterness in your heart, and it will keep you from being the leader God wants you to be.

Nehemiah endured it all: sarcasm, suspicion, gossip, mockery, threats, anonymous notes, false accusation. Remain patient and resilient through criticism. It is important to be firm in purpose without becoming cranky, vengeful, or mean-spirited. Cranky, vengeful, and mean-spirited pushes people away; it doesn't draw people to your vision.

If you are still waiting for justice from someone who wronged you in the past, move on! Don't give the wrongdoers in your life that kind of power over you. Step into your new season. Forgiveness can unlock those shackles and free you from being bound to the unkindness, thoughtlessness, or cruelty of another. Draw a line in the sand and say, 'today is the day I move on.'

Forgiveness Brings Restoration

The best example of this kind of forgiveness is Job, a man that the Bible describes as a nobleman, wealthy and righteous. But his circumstances, changed into severe calamity. He lost everything: his children, his marriage, and all his wealth. After some time, Job's friends came to comfort him, but concluded that his calamity was caused by nothing else but that he had sinned against God.

But God spoke to Job and commanded him to pray and forgive his friends. And the Bible says that the Lord restored to Job only after he had prayed for his friends—he restored all Job had lost and multiplied it. God gave Job twice as much as he had before. Faith only works through forgiveness. Many miracles in our life are waiting for us to release bitterness in our life. The Lord restored everything to Job after he had prayed for his friends (see Job 42:10). And Job died, old and full of days!

Peter asked how many times we should forgive—7 times? Jesus said 70 times 7. In other words, forgiveness is not about keeping score, but losing count. (see Matthew 18:22) And Matthew 6 says if you forgive others, your father will forgive you. If you refuse to forgive, God will not forgive your sin. Often, the people who hurt you the most are those you have helped and loved.

I drew a line in the sand by writing a letter of transition to the ULICAF Board and clearly stating, "I have moved on. It is time to move into forgiveness and the freedom it brings."

In summary, to forgive someone is to display reverence toward God. Forgiveness is not saying the one who hurt you was right. Forgiveness is stating that God is faithful, and He will do what is right! (see Proverbs 20:22) Ask God to increase your faith to forgive for your own restoration.

Leadership Lesson #6: Be Strong and Courageous

"Challenge and Courage" is the title I chose for this book!

Without courage your calling is crippled. Courage moves us from mere talk to action, from potential to actuality. Courage is essential to leadership because the first person to step out in a new direction is viewed as the leader.

Leaders who are making significant impact today are those who are making sacrifices and taking risks, confronting evils. Courage is not the absence of fear, but the commitment to confront and overcome it.

Joshua faced doubters who feared the Promised Land was too difficult to conquer. "Be strong and courageous," God instructed Joshua (Joshua 1:9 NIV).

Abraham left his home country to journey to a place he wasn't even sure existed. Why? Because God told him to.

Gideon led an army of only three hundred to defeat an army of thousands. (see Judges 7) Nehemiah overcame fierce opposition to rebuild the walls of Jerusalem in fifty-two days. (see Nehemiah 6:15)

The lives of great Christian leaders teach us that those who follow a God-sized calling need God-sized courage. They follow the words of the Psalm, "Be of good courage, and He shall strengthen your heart, all of you who hope in the Lord" (Psalm 31:24 NKJV).

I chose the title *Courage* for this book because I desire to push myself out of my comfort zone. Second, I desire to push those who will read this book out of their comfort zones in order to provoke them to grow for God. So, here is my single question for you, "what if you stepped into all God has created you to be?" I urge you to step out and take that first step, because we may never know the ripple effect of that one courageous decision. Your decision to do something courageous may result in something greater than you ever imagined.

Embedded in courage is an unswerving confidence in God. Nehemiah learned to have confidence in God, and never failed to remind the people of the Lord's presence and protection. Leaders who are authentic will consistently turn other's attention to the true source of strength—the One who can accomplish the impossible.

Occasionally, you might doubt your own ability; never doubt God's invincible commitment to His work! (see Hebrews 4:10–11)

So what does a courageous leader look like? Here are three characteristics:

1. Courageous leaders are committed to relentless growth. Are you hungry for growth? Strong leaders are deeply committed to growth, no matter how far they have climbed the ladder of success. They strive toward personal and spiritual improvement.

2. Courageous leaders are dedicated to ridiculous routines. Courageous leaders don't get tired of doing the same right thing over and over again.

3. Courageous leaders invest in resilient relationships. First, it requires deeper relationships with God and with fellow human beings. It is all about relationships that stand the test of time.

In summary, it is time for us to lead our families, organizations, and nations with courage. We must dream big and commit to the fulfillment of our dreams. We must stand with conviction for principles and the highest values at whatever cost. Future generations will be glad for our investment.

As a leader, your first expression of courage is to dream about what would be and could be. Then allow your mind to wander outside the boundaries of what is, and begin to create a mental picture of what could be. Years ago, I read and remembered a powerful little sentence: "Dream no small dreams, for they stir not the hearts of men."

Leadership Lesson 7: Draw Power from Christ-like Partners

Don't go it alone; look for others God will send to multiply your influence.

I was 57 years old when I transitioned from the ministry that my wife and I had led for more than 20 years. We ministered to Liberian refugees who fled their country during 14 years of civil conflict. We loved them and we were very successful. Then a new season arrived, and we had to move on. However, I was not satisfied to continue the same way strategically. I wanted to do greater things than we had ever accomplished previously. I wanted to believe and take Jesus at his word: "If you believe in me, you will do even greater things than I have done" (John 14:12 NIV).

At this start-up, we are focusing on recruiting new partners. We prayed and asked God to connect us with *new* partners who would make a *big* difference. People who possessed commitment upfront.

The greatest partnership effort we made came when our dear friend, Jon Lieberman, our youngest daughter Tonzia Buor, and five other gifted friends agreed to serve on our new board. The "seed" for the vision was planted in 2015. This group helped give birth to and named our organization Christian Leadership Training International (CLTI) and applied for the 501(c) 3 non-profit status.

I hope you find inspiration in the following stories of Christ-minded followers.

JON LIEBERMAN

Jon Lieberman is the Chairman of the CLTI Board of Directors and has held this position since its beginning in 2015. I first met Jon in 2002 at a Global Leadership Conference at Grace Church in Noblesville, Indiana. Jon and I both were members of Grace Church and I was involved in a Friday morning Bible study which Jon led for many years. As we became ready to announce the vision of CLTI, Jon was the first friend that I invited to help set up the board, apply for a non-profit status, and open our ministry's first bank account. Previous to joining CLTI, Jon served on the ULICAF board. Jon is an incredible leader and works alongside all members of our team to develop and grow our organization. Jon is my consultant on everything including writing and editing grant proposals and newsletters for CLTI. Jon has given generously and is a loyal supporter and encourager of my goals and vision with RICA.

Jon is a Jewish believer in the Messiah Jesus and has a business background in real estate for over 35 years. He is presently serving as a Messianic Jewish Bible teacher and is on the staff of Chosen People Ministries, an international Jewish Evangelism ministry.

MARK OEHLER

Mark Oehler has been a member of the CLTI Board of Directors since its beginning in 2015. I met Mark through a mutual friend. He helped edit my first book and co-authored the second book. Mark edited this third book, too. Mark graduated with a degree in mechanical engineering from the University of Washington. He became a Christian while in college. Mark has spent more than 30 years writing manuals, procedures, and training with the last 20 years at Eli Lilly in Indianapolis. Mark retired in November 2022. Mark has given generously and is a loyal supporter and encourager of my goals and vision with RICA. Mark and his wife Nicole reside in Carmel, Indiana.

LOUISE JAESCHKE

We first came to know Louise back in 1997 at Northwest Covenant Church in Mount Prospect, Illinois. There she had done newsletter editing in the past and has served in many capacities over the years. Louise is a retired registered nurse. As we were working to start CLTI, I received an email from Louise that said, "I am available if you need help with your newsletter editing." We were really in need! I responded by saying, "Please, we do need your help." Louise committed to serve as our newsletter editor. This was just her initial step. When Louise saw that we did not have a website, she offered to self-train on website development, and designed CLTI's website, plus helped me to write grant proposals.

TONZIA L. BUOR

Our daughter, Tonzia is the Vice President for Human Resources at TriStar Summit Medical Center in Nashville, Tennessee. Tonzia serves on the CLTI Board of Directors and specifically plays the role of CLTI's Communications Coordinator. She works alongside all members of our team to develop and update our website, edit and distribute newsletters and write or edit grant proposals for CLTI. She gives generously, matched by her company. She is my consultant on everything I do. Her wise counsel and her steadfast work on behalf of this ministry has made her a trusted and beloved partner.

LUANN BOOTS

LuAnn Boots took on the role of Customer Service Coordinator. LuAnn is responsible for receiving gifts and sending out acknowledgement letters to our donors. She originally met Yah through a ladies Bible study that met every Wednesday morning for two hours. They studied the Bible and prayed together for more than 10 years. Yah introduced LuAnn to me, and I encouraged her to take a role in supporting the ministry. LuAnn is married to Ron, and they reside in Indiana.

JILL KENDRAT

Jill Kendrat is a member of the CLTI Board of Directors and Treasurer. She attends Grace Church in Noblesville, Indiana, where she and I had met years earlier studying together in a leadership seminar. I had invited Jill for lunch with the goal of asking her to become a monthly supporter. She agreed to give monthly financial support. Due to Jill's friendly smile, we did not stop there. I asked, "Jill, what do you do?" She answered, "my background is business and nonprofit accounting." In fact, Jill holds a master's degree in business and has spent most of her career with nonprofit organizations. I explained to Jill that we have a very competent treasurer, but his company has transferred him to South Carolina. I asked Jill if she could serve our accounting need as a treasurer. Jill promised to talk to her husband, and in a few days would get back to me. She also requested telephone numbers of some of our team members in our organization.

A few days later, I made a follow up call, and she said yes. Jill let me know that she had contacted two or three of our team members and our Board Chair, and all had spoken very highly of our reputation and past accomplishments, and she was glad to join our team.

JAY SKINNER

Jay is the host of an internet show called "The Buyers & Sellers Show" which airs every Friday morning live at 10:35 am EST (US) on LinkedIn, YouTube, and Facebook. Jay and I both attended Grace Church in Noblesville, Indiana, and were involved in a Friday morning Bible study for several years. As our new ministry progressed, Jay visited us twice in Liberia. He has worked many years in sales and marketing. Jay has given generously and is a loyal supporter and encourager of my goals and vision with RICA. Jay also became our Networking Coordinator and connected us with others who continue to support our ministry monthly. His internet program found at www.TheJaySkinner.com provides his contact information.

JOE WILLIAMSON

Many years ago, Joe was preparing for a short-term mission trip to Nairobi. At the same time, I was in search of someone that could hand-deliver some sweaters to two Liberian pastors that were doing an internship with the Nairobi Chapel. He took the sweaters and upon his return we reconnected. During that meeting, he explained to me that there was a group of men he was leading in discipleship training on Saturday mornings. He invited me to join his group if I wanted to. I have been part of that group for over ten years. As of this writing, Joe is single-handedly supporting the discipleship ministry of CLTI in Liberia. When I wrote my first book, *No More War*, he purchased 50 copies of the book and sent them to his clients. One of the clients made a $50,000 donation toward the building of LICC!

DAVID KETCHUM

David Ketchum is the president and founder of Mission Resource International. I met David in Indianapolis before the CLTI ministry began. During our meeting, David explained that he was already involved in mission work in Ghana, working to support small businesses. David agreed to partner with me in Liberia. Currently, David is supporting our entrepreneurship ministry in Liberia.

Gifted with the right partners, we gained momentum quickly, and this allowed us to build our dream into an even bigger dream. Our partners made us better, multiplied our efforts, and enabled us to do best what we had set out to do. Each of our partners provided us their knowledge, wisdom, expertise, experience, influence, and potential.

BEN and LAURETTA PATTERSON

One couple we met at the beginning of our ministry and who are still involved with us is Reverend Ben and Mrs. Lauretta Patterson. We have known them for decades and they still multiply our influence. When the Pattersons moved to Santa Barbara, California, they took us with them in their hearts. Later, they connected us with their church. Currently we in full partnership with the Santa Barbara Community Church.

Multiplying Your Influence

These are stories of real people who are followers of Christ. I want you to learn what they have in common. The first thing they have in common is *courage*. No matter what your God-given vision is, they get in and fulfill their *calling*. Another thing they have in common is *commitment*—the commitment to take one step at a time. Everyone, when asked to join us or to give, said "YES." When God calls them to a step of faith, their consistent, trusting answer is always the same, "Yes, Lord, I will." Lastly, they are generous with their financial support. All of these people give generously to the work God has called them to partner with.

These are not all the stories. These were just the beginning blessings. God brought many new partners to provide generous financial support. These initial leaders and helpers were my immediate team, but there were many other great partners as well.

In our previous ministry, we did not have a clear picture of the individuals we needed to invite to be our partners. We invited some people that did not end up being the right fit. Because the picture was not clear, we allowed the wrong people to paint the picture for us. Unfortunately, they painted their own pictures. With this behind us, I chose new partners, but I did not base my invitations on what they said they could do. I prayed and chose people based on what their values are. So, I listed the following qualities we look for in prospective partners:

1. **People who want to make a big difference beyond themselves:** A great partnership takes place because two people have something to offer each other, and what they give and receive are equally valued. For this kind of partnership to work, I spend a lot of time connecting, communicating, and nurturing the relationships.

2. **People who can provide a high synergy:** Synergy is a kind of teamwork that enables the group to outperform the individual members in the team. We want team members that can work well with others.

3. **People who can multiply influence:** I learned to look for people who will multiply my influence. I arrived in America many years ago as a refugee. On arrival in Holland, Michigan, I made a great discovery. When I partnered with like-valued people, I went from increasing my influence to multiplying my influence.

In summary, don't try to do ministry alone. Look for others God will send to help. Where possible, don't depend on one source of support. Commit to building partnerships with godly friends and churches seeking to serve God in the global world.

Leadership Lesson #8: Anchor in your Convictions

Be committed to listening to God daily.

We are too familiar with the word "impossible." The road to successful ministry is littered with challenges. We know that doubts and fears will not benefit a ministry, and so it is important to overcome your doubts and fears to succeed.

In 2015, when I submitted my resignation to the mission organization I had founded and had worked for, I quickly realized the necessity of beginning all over again. I was overwhelmed with all the things that I thought would not work. First, I was too old to start anything new. Where would I find supporters to give adequately to a new ministry? My doubts went on and on. But I soon realized that if I let my doubts conquer my thinking, I would soon fail to achieve my God-given vision. I wouldn't even get started.

I am writing this book for people who want the proven principles that will make you courageous. The key to success is being willing to stake everything on those principles.

The Bible says, "I can do all things through Christ who strengthens me" (Phil 4:13 NKJV).

Add to that the wisdom we learn from Ezra and Nehemiah: Don't let doubters try and discourage you; be committed to listening to God daily. The Apostle Paul states:

> But what things were gain to me, these I have counted loss for Christ; … I press toward the goal for the prize of the upward call of God in Christ Jesus (Philippians 3:7–12 NIV).

In summary, every leader who succeeds in any undertaking must be willing to burn their bridges and cut off all sources of retreat, if necessary. By staying focused on the God-given goal, the true leader proceeds with a definite purpose.

Leadership Lesson #9: Befriend Wise People and Become Wise (Proverbs 13:20)

Seek wise and mature godly friends.

I am blessed to have had a number of wise friends and mentors throughout my life. Find a few people that believe in your vision but are not afraid to give you constructive criticism. You don't want only "Yes" people around you.

Back in 1986, I received my first international invitation to attend Billy Graham's itinerant evangelists conference in Amsterdam. More than 10,000 international evangelists attended. Mrs. Eugenia De Haas, an attendee from Orono, Maine, became my first "wise friend and partner in ministry." Eugenia was an international director for neighborhood Bible study. During our brief meeting, she recorded my voice (African accent) to take back to her husband who was a professor of Soil Science at a university in Maine.

In 1994, when an opportunity showed up to pursue my education in America, beginning at a seminary in Holland, Michigan, she connected me with Dr. Gordon and Mrs. Margaret Van Wylen, President of Hope College. The Van Wylens became our wise friends. They became our partners and mentors. They introduced me and my family to Christ Memorial Church. God, by his design, expanded our "wise friends circle and network."

By God's design, we met Rev. Ben and Mrs. Lauretta Patterson. Rev. Patterson was the Dean of Chapel of Hope College and Westmont College. Decades have passed and the Pattersons remain our lifelong friends and partners in ministry.

In 2019, Yah and I visited Ben and Lauretta in their home in Carpentaria, California. Ben had recently retired, so I was anxious to learn something new from a retired friend. He is a prayer warrior and a pastoral leader. I asked Ben, "What will you do now in your retirement? What is on your bucket list?"

"There is still one thing on my bucket list," he said. "I want to do for my children what no one else can ever do." Then he turned to me, "Sei, start now, do for your children what only you can do for them."

I pondered his advice and began to think of ways I could serve my children. This was a foreign idea for me since in Liberia a man would never think of serving others in his family. What are some of the things I've done for my children since that conversation?

When I visit one of them and we eat a meal together, I wash the dishes and take the trash out. I have learned that I can drive them to work and take their car and clean it inside and out. For my daughter, I take her car to be serviced because I don't want her to have car trouble or be unsafe. I helped Tonzia by breaking down all the cardboard boxes from things she bought to furnish her new home. I then rented a U-Haul to take them to the recycling place.

This may not sound like a lot to some people, but with my background, it is monumental. From my African perspective, fathers do not wash dishes or clean their children's cars or vacuum their children's homes. However, I feel great satisfaction in being able to do these things when I visit my children. I am not shamed and they are not embarrassed to ask me to help them. It also gives us more time together to talk and enjoy one another's company.

In 1997, we moved to Chicago to study at Loyola University. God blessed us and expanded our network of wise friends. We settled in Mount Prospect, IL, and became members of Northwest Covenant Church. We launched our first ministry, the United Liberia Inland Church Associates and Friends (ULICAF) during our years at NWCC. Louise and David Jaeschke, members at Northwest, are among our lifelong friends and partners in ministry. As I mentioned earlier, Louise serves as our newsletter editor and website manager. Dave is a retired civil engineer in water reclamation and has consulted with us in the construction of the high school building and clean water planning.

In 2002, I met Jon Lieberman at a Global Leadership Summit. Jon is currently the chairman of CLTI's Board of Directors. Over the years, we've made several wise friends including Mark Oehler (my team writer), LuAnn Boots, Jill Kendrat, Brad Elliot, Dan Farrell, and Jay Skinner. We have also made hundreds of other friends. These are just few of the wise friends we have and who are serving with us in the ministry.

I am writing this book for leaders who have a calling to enter ministry careers or other careers to serve the Lord. In your preparation to be a leader, seek wise and mature godly friends. As you spend time with them, you will become like them because their godly character will influence you. Please choose wisely. Conversely, if we spend time with unwise and immature people, we will tend to become like them.

The ability to motivate and draw ministry partners is very critical. Leaders should develop skills such as verbalizing ideas, creating ambitious dreams and articulating goals succinctly. Leaders who motivate always inspire others to do and be their very best.

In summary, recruit and build a network of wise people who add synergy to your life's mission and vision. Look for people who will make a lifelong commitment to you. Look for those who will stick with you through the ups and downs of life. Remember also to be as good a friend to them as they are to you.

Leadership Lesson #10: Be Confident, but Flexible and Practical

Be alert for unexpected turns in the road and prepare to adjust.

As a leader, I learned to be flexible and practical, and to have a balanced grip on reality. It was the only way I could adapt to the leadership challenges I faced.

While every good and visionary leader has great dreams and ideas, he or she must move on with convictions and decisive action. Wise leaders understand that strategies that work well today might not work well tomorrow, and they need to recognize quickly when to change strategies. The leader must be proactive and continue developing new skills and approaches to problems before the need arises. Be alert for unexpected turns in the road.

Nehemiah instructed his workers to stay at their jobs. He, at the same time, wisely stationed others to protect the walls from attack. Nehemiah was a discerning man, and when he saw a problem, he acted quickly without over-reacting. Good leaders maintain that needed balance between staying positive and being aware of the negative.

In summary, Nehemiah's message is clear: Be aware of the landscape and know how you might need to adjust to meet the turns in the road of your life or ministry!

Leadership Lesson # 11: When the Bottom Falls Out, Earnestly Look to God for What is Next for You

Give God the broken pieces and let Him write the rest of the story.

You know my story by now. I put 20 years into ULICAF and then it abruptly ended.

If you keep following the light of God's presence through this dark and difficult world, you will see God turn around your impossible messes!

That is His promise! Nothing can stop the amazing redemptive power of our God. Let me illustrate this with a fun story.

The story is told of the Emperor of China. The Emperor of China had a problem. Something was destroying his mulberry trees. So, he did what any brilliant man does when faced with a problem he can't handle: he turned it over to his wife!

When Empress Ce Ling Shee looked at the trees, she noticed a moth laying eggs on the mulberry leaves. These eggs, of course, hatched into caterpillars. After a few days, each caterpillar spun a thread that it wrapped itself in, forming a cocoon.

The empress plucked one of the cocoons from the leaves and dropped it in hot water. Slowly, the delicate and beautiful thread began to unwind. It was a half mile long when the empress stretched it out and measured it! Then the thought occurred to her that perhaps this thread could be woven into cloth.

And that was the moment the silk trade was born. An empire of extraordinary beauty and wealth began with an emperor's garden disaster! [1]

I don't know if this story is true, but it makes the point that God often works wondrous good out of what seems to be bad.

Like everyone else, leaders sometimes might find it difficult to envision a positive outcome when in the middle of a mess. We look out onto the garden of our lives, find it in ruins, and feel helpless. We don't even know where to begin to make things right. How could the emperor have ever imagined that beauty and blessing could rise out of the thing that seemed to be the destruction of his beloved trees?

But making beautiful endings out of impossible situations is God's specialty. He never wastes a single trial. He transforms it all for our good and His glory.

Read these words from 1 Peter:

In all this you greatly rejoice, though now for a little while you may have had to suffer grief in all kinds of trials. These have come so that the proven genuineness of your faith — of greater worth than gold… may result in praise, glory and honor when Jesus Christ is revealed (1 Peter 1:6–7 NIV).

His promises:

We know that in all things God works for the good of those who love Him, who have been called according to His purpose (Romans 8:28 NIV).

The Spirit of the Sovereign Lord is on me because the Lord has anointed me… to bestow on them a crown of beauty instead of ashes, the oil of joy instead of mourning, and a garment of praise instead of a spirit of despair (Isaiah 61:1, 3 NIV).

Consider it pure joy, my brothers, and sisters, whenever you face trials of many kinds, because you know that the testing of your faith produces perseverance. Let perseverance finish its work so that you may be mature and complete, not lacking anything (James 1:2–4 NIV).

I will repay you for the years the locusts have eaten (Joel 2:25 NIV).

Blessed are you when people hate you, when they exclude you and insult you and reject your name as evil, because of the Son of Man. Rejoice in that day and leap for joy, because great is your reward in Heaven. For that is how their ancestors treated the prophets (Luke 6:22–23 NIV).

The enemy may throw every weapon he has at you, but he is not the one who gets to write the end of your story. God writes the end of the story.

In summary, give Him all the pieces of whatever has been broken. God is the only one who can make something beautiful out of it.

Leadership Lesson #12: Finish the Task

Success does not always come easily. As a leader, learn to develop the discipline to finish the task you are called to.

Good leaders are finishers! Keep trying until you and your group succeed. *A good leader knows how to concentrate on essentials without allowing perfectionistic details to block the path.* If you are engaged in construction like we are, some of the wall's stones will be crooked and a few of the joints may get loose. Maybe some things are not perfect, but get over it and keep moving to the end! To finish the task or project requires extraordinarily hard work and boundless unselfishness.

To finish well, godly leaders prevent themselves from being distracted. When we started the construction and development of Riverview International Christian Academy in Liberia, my wife and I made the decision to move closer to the frontlines. We sold our home in the US and moved our furniture to Liberia. Upon arrival in Liberia, we resolved to be on the project site every day, and no amount of distraction would get us to lose sight of our vision and plan.

The disciple John shared an insightful story that is worth our attention. When Jesus talked with the Samaritan woman, he was performing the will of God and received greater satisfaction than any mere physical food or water could offer him. Obedience to and dependence upon God's will summed up Jesus' whole life. God's will for Him was to finish the work the Father had given him to do. (see John 4:32–34).

191

Nehemiah, like many biblical leaders, pursued his goals with *commitment, careful planning, strategic delegation, focus on the task at hand and a continual reliance on God.* At every turn, Nehemiah was threatened by enemies from without and within, but conferred in prayer with God, placing every decision before Him. Nehemiah succeeded in completing the walls in 52 days because he never lost sight of the reason for the work and the source of power with which to accomplish the task (see Nehemiah 5:14; 6:3–10).

And when the task is finished, good leaders celebrate and have fun! In our case, we will have a blast, marching and dancing, shouting and singing. What a grand and glorious party to anticipate! I cannot wait to invite the President of Liberia to see the beauty of this unique facility. It's one of its kind in Liberia. I cannot wait to invite all, yes, all our American partners to join us for this celebration—it will be grand!

In summary, be a leader known for finishing what you've started. Do the best you can, but know perfection is sometimes unattainable. When you do finish and reach your goal, invite those who have helped you and celebrate.

Conclusion

Christ's followers must be Christian leaders with biblical character. Ezekiel recorded God's search for leaders who would "stand in the gap in the wall of righteousness so I wouldn't have to destroy the land," but, tragically, He "found no one" (Ezekiel 22:30 NIV). God's search continues today. Let's determine to be the women and men for whom God is searching to stand in the gap. Let's be the Nehemiah, Joshua, and Moses of this generation—Christians who get things done for God's glory, standing strong on rock-solid principles of leadership.

Part 8

Looking Ahead

Chapter 22: My Next Journey

Point of Decision

In August of 2013, I had the opportunity to attend the Global Leadership Summit telecast at Grace Church, Noblesville, Indiana. General Colin Powell (former U.S. Secretary of State) was among the speakers and was terrific. I purchased his latest book, *It Worked for Me: In Life and Leadership*, for details on his talk. In the seventh chapter, I was struck by a unique heading: "Where on the Battlefield?" (p. 196)

The General shared his experience about an insightful letter he had received from an older United States Ambassador Kennan. In the letter, Ambassador Kennan reminded the new Secretary of State of the Founding Father's intention around the two principal functions of the Secretary of State. First, the Secretary must function as the "President's most intimate and authoritative advisor on all aspects of American foreign policy." Second, the Secretary was to "exercise administrative control over the State Department and the Foreign Service." The letter then concludes, "You cannot properly perform either of these duties if you are constantly running around the world in your airplane."

On reflection, General Powell realized that Ambassador Kennan's letter was about finding the right balance in life. Where should the commander (strategic leader) of an organization be on the battlefield? The answer is: "where he can exercise the greatest influence and be close to the 'Point of Decision'." The location of the "Point of Decision," as Colin explains, is a function of a leader's experience, self-confidence, confidence in his people, and the needs of his superior. For me, the leader's "Point of Decision" is the place where I can best see what is really going on, best influence the outcome, and yet also still be available to God (my superior) for His direction. The prophet Micah wrote:

He has showed you, O mortal [man], what is good. And what does the Lord require of you? To act justly and to love mercy and to walk humbly with your God (Micah 6:8 NIV).

For RICA, three of my goals at the "Point of Decision" are to (1) provide the strategic leadership RICA needs to grow into a reputable college prep high school in Liberia, (2) remain committed to networking with my friends and partners (existing and new) to develop the necessary financial resources needed to finish building RICA and (3) develop the leaders (new and existing) who will sustain RICA far into the future.

What is next for me? Now that RICA is up and running, I do not intend to rest on my laurels. I like the words of the Apostle Paul on this:

Not that I have already obtained all this, or have already been made perfect, but I press on to take hold of that for which Christ Jesus took hold of me. Brothers, I do not consider myself yet to have taken hold of it. But one thing I do: Forgetting what is behind and straining toward what is ahead, I press on toward the goal to win the prize for which God has called me heavenward in Christ Jesus (Philippians 3:12–14 NIV)

I do know (or at least believe in faith) that I will always be involved with RICA. Practically, there are things like fundraising that will likely benefit from my involvement for the foreseeable future. I have worked diligently to establish RICA. I am passionate about telling our story well.

I look forward to continuing to tell people about RICA and share my passion for education and educating Liberian youth.

What is God telling me about my future? I'm not completely sure. I do not hear loud prophetic voices, but only the still, quiet voice—and that only occasionally. For much of God's plan, just like most Christians, I must wait for the right time and circumstances to provide some direction. Often, it is the closed doors that have directed me to a path left open, a path that has taken me closer to the fruition of God's plan for my life. I do know this from my study of God and His Word: God will take what we give Him and use it to His glory. I believe, in faith, He wants to expand our work in Liberia. For God to do so, it will take full commitment and trust in Him. If we continue with that level of commitment and trust, He will continue to bless us.

Mentoring

I want to finish well the race that is set before me, so one thing I need to do is more mentoring. I think of this prayer in Psalms:

> When I am old and gray headed, O God, do not forsake me
> until I declare your strength to this generation, your power
> to everyone who is to come (Psalm 71:18 NKJV).

I am committed to live for the next generation. The wisdom is that when you live only for your own generation, your vision will perish. We need to concern ourselves with those leaders who will follow us. I do not have to look far. Some of the best leaders to be trained are among my students at RICA. One day they will take the high school that trained them to the next level. I would envision some of our students pursuing further studies abroad, returning to Liberia, and serving Riverview in various positions—even as the Principal or Vice Principal of Academic Affairs, or campus pastors.

I would like to spend more time coaching and inspiring the next generation. I would like to spend more time helping young students. I want to help them go further than I have. I want to help them build a Liberia in their lifetime that is even greater than the one I believe I will see during my life on this earth.

And this is possible. God used a man of God to bring me to Him. Then God changed my life and taught me how to share my faith with others so that some would come to believe in Jesus as their Savior. The Lord is changing their lives as they follow Him and become the future leaders in Liberia.

Discipling

Jesus commissioned his followers:

All authority has been given to me in heaven and on earth. Go therefore and make disciples of all the nations, baptizing them in the name of the father and of the Son and of the Holy Spirit and teaching them to observe all things that I have commanded you; and lo, I am with you always, even to the end of the age (Matthew 28: 8–19 NKJV).

Currently, I meet weekly with several high school students at my house and disciple them just as Jesus commanded. I started with a few young men, and now the group has grown to more than 50. Some of the students are now trained to disciple other groups in different communities in and around Gompa. I am praying and planning to take our discipleship further—even **beyond Liberia.**

Sustainability

So, even though my love for RICA is unabated, I also am working to make RICA sustainable even when I am less involved. Regardless of other plans, I will not live forever, and RICA will go on after my time has passed. This is the reason that CLTI, like other organizations, does succession planning. RICA is a community effort; it is not a one-man show. It is the sum of all our work for many years and the many sacrifices that we made to make this dream a reality. So, I continue to prepare people for service in God's work. My hope is that they prepare the generation after themselves, so that they too will become disciples of Christ and pass on to the next generation what is entrusted to them. Through faith, the vision for RICA is to be a source of Liberian Christian leaders for years to come.

God called me to do this work. He prepared me to do this work in ways I did not understand at the time. I think of all my schooling! I loved school, but it seemed never-ending at times. Without it, I could never have helped to shape this dream or lead RICA through its beginning and heavy growth stage. Only God knew what I would need. Yet, I am also helping Him prepare others so that they will carry on our dream. So, at some point, there will be a time—or several times—of transition as I let go of some of my duties at RICA.

Open to God's Leading

For my part, I need to think about what is next. The vision of RICA has been so much a part of me for so long that is hard to imagine anything else. So I continue to serve God at RICA, but I also remain open to His leading. It is hard to know how or where God will lead next, but I know I need to be open to opportunities.

Now is not a time for retirement, but soon may be a time to rise to the next challenge. Whatever God calls me to, I will work to do it well for His glory and so finish well the race before me.

It is not good to place restrictions on God. For one thing, sometimes it seems like He delights in assigning us to duties we say we loathe (that He might show us He works even there). However, and I say this to my reader and myself, we should let go of preconceived notions of what God wants us to do. This is a matter of trust. There is nothing but that we should trust God. He will never lead us astray. He will lead us only to what is right. He will not call us to do anything that cannot work out for good in the long run. My Christian friends, you know the verse as well as I do:

> And we know that in all things God works for the good of those who love him, who have been called according to his purpose (Romans 8:28 NIV).

So, again, I say this to myself as well as my readers: do not put restrictions on what God wants to do with your life. Work to have a conviction that you will do what God wants you to do. God rarely calls us to a work or career we truly hate; He will, however, call us to a work or ministry we find difficult or uncomfortable, or one that we think is beneath educational level.

I am a life-long learner. I have been in school most of my youth and adult life. And even though I may no longer be a registered student at a particular school, I want to continue learning. I like reading good books and, hopefully, I can write some more books. Scripture reading will be a discipline of mine for life. I am to "lead diligently." How does one lead diligently when there is so much to read and learn? I want to constantly get better at leading people at our institution, and the only way to do that is to become a voracious reader. When you read, you get new ideas and new ways of doing things.

In his book, *Half Time: Changing Your Game Plan from Success to Significance*, Bob Buford explained the importance of second half learning (the 2nd half of your life). According to Buford, in the first half of our lives, learning is focused on career and success. In the second half, learning becomes focused on "unlearning the doctrine of specialization."

My second half learning will move me toward a more holistic approach to leadership and to the world. It will also demand more of me. When the mind is empty, there can be many distractions. So, I will continue to concentrate on learning good and wholesome things to protect my mind from the debasing things that are easily absorbed.

What to learn is another important question for me. First, I believe continuing to study the Bible is extremely important. The Bible was written by 40 human authors under the supernatural inspiration of God and is our authority for all matters of faith and practice. I have been reading and studying the Bible for years. I have read the entire Bible several times. Even so, I continue to learn new things from it.

Second, I want to learn anything that will help me accomplish this mission God has called me to do. Because I am heading and developing a newly established academic institution, I will make use of conferences, workshops, seminars, and study in the areas of business, technology, management, leadership, and related subjects.

I am a pastor. I have been performing some type of work in the church almost since I became a Christian. So, if an opportunity in business presented itself, should I ignore it out of hand? At one time in my life, my answer would have been "yes": yes, I should ignore what I would have felt was a "temptation." I was working and studying to become a better pastor, not a businessman. Today, I see it differently. I would pray and then ask for God to give me discernment.

Let me be more specific. I would ask for discernment between what is right and what is almost right. What the world knows as the best choice may be what is almost right in the sight of God and, therefore, is to be refused (so we can do what is right and best in God's eyes). For me, being able to make more money, or even much more money, would not be the deciding issue. However, impacting people's lives is not exclusive to pastors. A businessman can impact the lives of many people also. The decision would not be about money, but about following God's plan for my life. The deciding issue would be whether this is what God wants me doing next.

I am a teacher. I have taught at many different levels in my life from grade school to college. I am a Christian teacher; I believe in sharing God's word. My love of soul-winning and discipleship stems from personal experience. It was Dr. Amos Miamen who, for the very first time, clearly introduced me to the possibility of eternal life. That introduction created the spark that lit that flame of a revolution that swept the Holy Spirit into my life and gave me new life. Dr. Miamen's work did not stop with this introduction but was followed by several years of mentoring. It is amazing that even to this date, he has never stopped calling to check on me and to find out how Yah and the children are doing. He reminds me constantly how his own faith is still growing or how his faith has come under attack, but how God by His grace, has delivered him and given him peace.

I love philosophy because it stimulates our thinking. I want to encourage our students coming to RICA to think beyond obtaining an education for a career. I believe in every Christian's heart a spark is glowing. If fed and nurtured it will become a glowing fire for Christ. I want to be able to light fires in these young men and women. That is the energy I see in the eyes of young Liberian students, and my prayer is that they will have the courage to live the dreams that God has placed within them.

I am reminded of Jesus and Simon's story described by the Apostle Luke. Prior to the encounter, Simon had been engaged in a small family fishing business venture and had been loyal to that tradition. But then Jesus approached him, and asked Simon to cast his net into the deep water. Despite Simon's experience as evidenced by the night-long struggle for a catch, he immediately obeyed Jesus' command and let the net down into the deep water. Instantaneously, his new faith was rewarded with a "great catch"—so great that he had to seek help to secure the fish onboard. And the new experience transformed Simon into a "fisher of men instead of fish" (see Luke 5:1). The lesson: In many ways, we are like Simon with past experience which is sometimes the barrier that stops us from moving forward. But when we let go of our experience and let faith takes its place, we too can be rewarded and transformed to do greater things.

Does all this mean I should only work for a Christian school? Again, you know the answer to this as well as I do. If I worked in the Education Ministry for the Government of Liberia or for one of its counties, I would have the opportunity to impact many more students that I can today at RICA. Working for the government would place me in a position where I would have to deal more regularly with politics and be more publicly known. While I am the face of RICA to the outside world, I do not think of this as one of my strengths. My current political involvement is listening to the news and trying to understand where my country is going next. However, I need to remain open to where God may lead. You do too.

Currently, I am the founder and CEO of RICA. There is a fully functional administrative staff that is led by a principal. We need to pray and seek the mind of the Lord. God is trying to bring good to Liberia. God is trying to help Liberians live in peace and recover economically. God is working in Liberia through more than just RICA. Neither do I feel like it is beneath my dignity to go from being a big fish in a small pond to a small fish in a large pond. RICA is not the only high school in Liberia; many high schools and colleges are springing up and older ones are growing. I need to be open to going where God leads even if it is to a place I had not thought God would find a way to use me.

I am a Liberian by birth. I grew up in Liberia and I have spent most my adult life working to help Liberia or other countries in West Africa. It makes human sense that God would use me that way. These are my people. Even so, should I put a restriction on God, saying, "Let me serve you anyway you think best, Lord, but only if it is in Liberia"? I think the right (and even best) answer is obvious to both of us. I am committed to my countrymen, but I have travelled widely since my youth and I will tell you something we all know deeply in our hearts, even though from time to time we ignore it. All people are the same in at least this: They have a deep and abiding need for God. I know that many ignore this. For that matter, I know that many ignore this for their whole lives, no matter how much the Holy Spirit convicts or how much their Christian friends and relatives share with them. Knowing that the fields are ripe for harvest all over the world, should I place a restriction on God's path for me? Again, we know the answer to this as Christians. Even though it might lead to an uncomfortable path, I need to be open to going anywhere in the world that God might call me to minister.

This is somewhat hard for me. The reason is simple. Though it was often confusing on the journey, looking back I can see how God worked in my life to bring me to the place I am today as founding President of RICA. God has called me in this time (the end of the 20th century and beginning of the 21st century) and place (United States and Liberia) and He gave me the resources I would need to fulfill that role. From my youngest days, He grew me in specific ways. It is true I had a passion for learning (God given); it is true I worked and studied very hard; however, it is also true He gave me many opportunities to study and improve my education. He directed my path and provided a way when, sick of school, I went on to get a PhD at Loyola.

There are good biblical examples of God calling people to a specific people and context as well. Moses? He was called to lead the Jews out of Egypt, not lead or help lead the Egyptian nation as might have been the case with his upbringing in Pharaoh's household. (Exodus chapter 3) The Apostle Paul? He was called to be the Apostle to the Gentiles and not the Jews even though his training was to be a top rabbi.

My first duty is not even to Liberia. My first duty is to God and the universal church of all believers. If I want God's presence to go with me night and day, then I need to be walking the path God has laid before me. If God's plan for me includes working in ministry in some place in the world other than Liberia, then I need to be open to that leading. It is true I am more comfortable living and working in Liberia and United States. It is true I seem to have been preparing all my life for this role as founding President of RICA. It is also true that many of the skills I have developed and many of my experiences can be transferred to other locations, situations, and peoples. God is a God of miracles and of mystery, and of great love for all people. I will stay in Liberia if that is what He wants me to do, but I will go elsewhere if God gives me a vision to advance His kingdom.

Chapter 23: An Invitation to Visit (or Return)

We look forward to our friends, many of whom supported us in the work of LICC, seeing how RICA is working to transform the lives of Liberian children and their community.

My Personal Invitation to You

I make my personal invitation to you: Consider visiting RICA. Some of you may have visited LICC, so please prayerfully consider coming back to Liberia to see RICA. We look forward to meeting you. For our Christian friends, we look forward to sharing the fellowship that is common to all believers.

What You Will See If You Visit RICA

First of all, you will meet Liberians. Andrew Taylor is British. He is a research fellow in Michigan. Andrew and I shared a room during my trip to Israel several years ago. Each night, we had conversations of all sorts before going to bed. One night, I invited Andrew to visit LICC and perhaps teach a course. His quick question was, "Sei, if I come to Liberia, what will I see?" I immediately supplied the answer, "Andrew, you will see 'People.'" What I actually meant was that when you come to Liberia you will meet some of the friendliest people on earth. I know this sounds like I am blowing my own trumpet (or at least Liberia's).

However, Liberians are even more unabashedly friendly to strangers than their own fellow Liberians! In the 1990s, an Anglican Bishop in Uganda took me into his home and refused to allow anyone to accommodate me but himself. He behaved that way because when

President Idi Amin was killing Ugandans, the bishop had escaped to Liberia where he had been treated wonderfully.

Hopefully you will find, like most visitors do, that Liberians are a friendly and social people. Although there are 16 distinct tribes, you will probably not be aware of that and will see us all simply as Liberians.

Just like with LICC, RICA started with a stretch of partly forested barren ground. That land was dedicated to the hope for a better life for our children and their children's children.

Now if you come to visit, you will see a functioning preparatory high school (grades 1 through 12). We have classrooms with students. When you come, you will see a school that is reaching out to Liberians in the local community. You will see a well-designed campus layout beautifully crafted and landscaped. You will see our fish ponds! You will see fruit trees and, in season, enjoy some of those fruits with us at our dinner table.

You will also see a school in progress. In fact, do not be surprised to see piles of bricks waiting to be used in some new construction project!

The most important thing you will witness is students who are trying to build a better future for themselves and their community. Many hope that RICA will give them the education they need to go on to college. They will be there to study and learn and to meet people. And they will welcome you and want to get to know you.

A Snapshot of Liberia

If you come to visit, you will see more than RICA. You will have the chance to see Liberia. As a country that was founded with help from the United States of America, whose capital was named for an

American president, James Monroe, many of the Liberian institutions were inspired by American institutions. There still is a lasting American influence in Liberia.

As far as weather, our dry season is from October through May, and rainy season starts in June and goes through September. The split between dry and wet seasons is about 60/40. We have about six or seven months of dry weather and about five or six months of rainy weather. The dry season is when we do most of our construction work. We plant during the rainy season. This is partly because rain is very important to growing rice. In April we get some rain, but not too heavy, so we can plant corn and other vegetables. The heavy rains typically begin in July and go through September. Therefore, we plant rice in early May. In August through September there is very heavy rain and we wait for the crops to grow. From the end of October into November is our harvest time. Besides rice, we like to eat meat and fish. Wild animal meat, when available, is a particular delicacy.

When you come to Liberia, you will see a land of hope and optimism. You will also see a Liberia that is still recovering from the civil war. The main focus of the average Liberian is the personal struggle to put food on the table and keep a roof over their family's heads. After that, they are focused on various things going on in Liberia, as well as hoping for continued development in their country.

The need for continued development is real. For example, Liberia has a population of four million people, but we have only 150 doctors! So increasing the number of Liberian healthcare workers is a big focus. Although modern roads continue to be built, many of these roads are still primitive. It can take quite a while to go from one place to another. The government of Liberia is focused on building roads, bridges, and other infrastructure.

Investment is pouring into Liberia. Now that the rule of law is prevalent again, outside businesses feel safe to invest in various start-up endeavors. Over 16 billion dollars (U.S. dollars) has been put into Liberia and more is expected to follow.

Little outside news gets to the average Liberian. This lack of knowledge about the outside world is partially because of the lack of current technology. There are few TVs in Liberia. For example, in Monrovia, our most developed city, about 5% of the population have TVs. Even Internet access is restricted as it costs $50 a month for unlimited access. Compared to the United States or Canada, there are few news sources.

Cell phones are very popular with those who can afford them. It is relatively cheap to call from Liberia to America—it is more expensive to call Liberia from America. Radios (FM, and short-wave) are relatively common, so some news and information gets distributed that way.

Along with several other African countries, Liberia has a low per capita Gross Domestic Product. Often it is less than $1,000 a year. With continued development and recovery from the civil war, the average Liberian's standard of living is expected to change. Even without GDP increasing, the safety that peace has brought has measurably improved the lives of all Liberians.

In our Liberian churches you will find passionate people who love Christ and work to share their faith with their community. Although my viewpoint is skewed somewhat by having attended mostly large churches while in American, I should mention that most Liberian churches are small. It is difficult to get enough money to build large ones. However, like in America, they are affiliated with each other through denominations.

What Past Visitors Have Said

My friend Richard Rath visited Riverview in 2022 to teach physics. Rich is originally from Rochester, New York, but lives now in Denver. Rich teaches physics at the senior high level. He is also helping us to set up our first physics and chemistry lab.

Here is a summary of his visit in his words:

A VISIT TO RIVERVIEW INTERNATIONAL CHRISTIAN ACADEMY AND LIBERIA

This astounding adventure began for me in February 2018 when I volunteered to assist with the initial evaluations leading to the design of this unique school. As has been carefully documented and presented elsewhere, this school has literally arisen from the Liberian forest totally by God's Hand through the faith and vision of its founder, Dr. Sei Buor, a native of the area where the school has been established. The school is located in the southern outskirts of the city of Ganta, Liberia in Nimba County. Ganta is the second-largest city in Liberia. At present, the school has over 450 students enrolled. The building is designed for 1,500 students and their teachers.

This visit is the result of a series of short conversations with my wife Johanna, who, sadly, was taken to Jesus before our intentions could be fulfilled. After she died, and because of her interest, I decided to proceed with the trip to honor her memory. She had said several times in 2020 and early 2021 that it would be nice to go and teach during the first days of the school's opening and a trip was thus planned for departure from the U.S. in late August, 2021. Because of unavoidable delays, departure occurred on March 21, 2022.

As intended, I have come to assist with the teaching of physics to 10th and 11th graders. In the four classes, I have been privileged to team-teach with Mr. Wellington Patrick, a Liberian native, gifted teacher and engineer. 105 (29-10A, 31-10B, 23-11A, 22-11B) students, ranging in age from 13 to 17, populate these classes. Their collective attitude is one of respect and interest. They are, however, typical teen-agers! Exuberance, haste, inattention and other distractions plague them, just as in other schools. But, in general, they are excited to be in an environment where genuine, caring people teach rigorous and thorough lessons, founded upon Biblical principles. The physics program is one year, and, in an orderly way, presents the topics of classical physics, from the consideration of issues related to physical properties measurements, force and energy balances and extends to those associated with heat, light, electrical and other forms of energy.

It is deeply gratifying to have students visit my office to ask questions and seek advice. In my experience with teens in the U.S., I recall only sparse advice questions or discussion. An example from Ganta: A ninth-grader, age 13 came to my office with one of his classmate friends. Though he is in the process of applying to the school's extra-curricular engineering-acquaintance program, he declared to me that he is studying to become a gynecologist. His earnestness convinced me quickly that he is focused on his goal. I asked if he'd practice in Liberia.

He quickly said no, then, after I reminded him of his Spiritual connection, that he ought to "give back," like Dr. Buor has, he quickly reconsidered and we talked about how he could "give back" without being overwhelmed. His grace was beyond his years. I've not met many 13-year-olds so mature and gracious.

The school is in session from 7:30 AM to 4:00 PM, (in the Greenwich Mean Time zone), with 1-hour classes. The students remain in their rooms. Teachers move between rooms on each hour. A noon recess of 1-hour provides a lunch break and rest. The school operates on a 10-month schedule, paralleling the Liberian public school system. COVID-19 caused the opening last fall to be delayed until November 1. Thus, this school year will end in August.

It has been an exciting challenge to teach in a building that loudly echoes the clamor of hundreds of students chattering while awaiting the beginning of the next class, and to lecture in classrooms with only natural lighting available. After coming from cool Colorado, the 80° to 95°F temperatures were a welcome change. The cool breezes in the early evening are refreshing. Not having electric power consistently or continuously has also made the experience memorable. Probably the most heart-warming has been the interaction with the students, teachers and staff, both in the classroom and after school. I have fallen in love with the Liberians. The kids call me either Uncle Rich or Mr. Rich, at my instruction just after I arrived.

Each school day, commendably, the children all line up in front of the school and salute the Liberian flag and sing their national anthem. This is always followed by a thoughtful devotional by the school chaplain. After the devotional, a prayer is lifted to Our LORD, often led by one of the students. Such activities truly stir my heart. The opening begins at 7:30 AM; classes start promptly at 8.

Motorbikes, this time of year (the dry season), outnumber mosquitos. Since arrival, up to the writing of this note, I have not seen one mosquito. However, motorbikes in Liberia are as numerous as taxis in New York City. I have even seen a five-passenger motorbike with an awning, no less!

The Liberian food is delicious! Rice is an important staple and is combined in both colorful and tasty ways with garden egg (alias, eggplant), steamed cassava leaves, fish, chicken, beef, goat, cabbage and other delights. Roasted plantain is also a tasty treat, and "street food," that is, charcoal-roasted corn-on-the-cob is widely enjoyed by everyone. The pineapple is straight from heaven along with the sweet, delectable bananas, and mangos (they are "everywhere" this time of year). I think the pineapple here is the best I've ever tasted."

My Fellow Expatriates

The work of Liberian International Christian College and now RICA would not have happened without the involvement of expatriate Liberians. I may have led both those efforts, but it was the work of many, many Liberians that created the end results, including the two schools. I am thankful for every one of you, whether your efforts were small or large. We helped improve the lives of Liberians. We helped make Liberia a better place.

Yet, when I am talking to local Liberian leaders in government, the church, or business, they sometimes ask me what we can do to get more expatriates involved in development in Liberia. They have asked me how we can find more people who will sacrificially lead. Yes, we need people who will contribute money and visit. But we need as many people who will volunteer and coordinate others to tackle larger projects.

If you are an expatriate Liberian or the child of an expatriate, I would ask you to prayerfully consider your involvement with your home country. Perhaps, your calling is to support the work of others. If so, thank you for all you will do. For some of you, however, God will call you to do more. There is much that remains to be done! There are children to educate, church communities to grow, businesses to be created, and infrastructure to build. Perhaps, you are one of the people who will inspire others to take on these large types of projects.

Dr. Peter and Mrs. Julie Nehsahn are among our most generous monthly financial donors and sustainability partners. Dr. Nehsahn is Senior Pastor of Caring Believers Fellowship Church in Atlanta, Georgia.

Liberian officials at Riverview dedication

Thomas Doe Nah
Commissioner General

Thomas Doe Nah with team and Sei

Thomas Doe Nah is Commissioner General of the Republic of Liberia, making him one of the top government officials in Liberia. He granted RICA 100% duty-free importation on whatever is shipped into Liberia

216

for the school. He personally gave 500 bags of cement toward the construction of the cafeteria, and he frequently visits the campus to give encouragement. He is really, really passionate about RICA.

US delegation to Riverview dedication

Visiting trainers and Ganta border Immigration Commander

Visiting trainers helping our staff

Tonzia Buor (Nashville, TN) and Nenplenseh
Wahkeleh (Pensacola, FL)

Chapter 24: A Hundred Years from Now

One of the biggest mistakes we make is thinking in terms of one generation. It is not only shortsighted, but it's also selfish. Some think that what God does for us is only for our benefit. God does want to bless us, but He also wants a legacy that extends to the third and fourth generations. God has shown us throughout the Bible that actions taken by one individual are meant to impact generations to come. We think right here and what is happening locally, but God is thinking nations and worldwide and generations.

The key to dreaming big is thinking long term. And the bigger the dream is, the longer the timeline needs to be. If you are thinking in terms of eternity, you should have some dreams that can't be accomplished in your lifetime.

Richard Arthurs is one of RICA's young and brilliant agriculture instructors for the junior and senior high levels. He graduated from the University of Liberia with a BSC degree in Sustainable Agriculture.

Whenever Richard sees my car parked, he takes the opportunity to update me on local politics and other current events. One day I was visiting RICA's chapel construction site and he walked in. He asked me to turn around as he had something very important to share with me. He explained that the chapel space was not adequate for large gatherings. When I attempted to argue my case, he explained that RICA started small, but its population will grow immensely in the future. When I failed to convince him, I asked what the solution was since the building was already at the window level. I wondered what we could we do to expand the space. He explained that we do not need to add or break down anything, but we need to create a second floor that would allow us to double the seating capacity as needed.

The week following my conversation with Richard, I heard a speaker who chose his text from John 4:5–10. His sermon title was "Living for the Next Generation." He explained how Jacob's well endured to Jesus' day (hundreds of years later) and never ceased to be a blessing from generation to generation as the people continued to glorify God for its provision.

Then the lights came on. I asked myself, "What is God teaching from this message and the conversation with Richard?" Putting these two events together, I asked myself, "How can building RICA be a continued blessing from generation to generation for at least 100 years?"

RICA cafeteria (left), gym (center), and chapel with upper floor (right)

Chapel showing the second floor

What are you doing today that will make a difference 100 years from now? Every generation must steward what's been entrusted to them. It starts with honoring the generation that has gone before us by learning everything we can from them. But that is only half the equation when it comes to passing along a multi-generational blessing. It continues by empowering the generation that comes after us. That is how the baton of blessing is passed to the third and fourth generation. And that is what the Psalmist advocated:

> So the next generation would know them [the acts and laws of God], even the children yet to be born, and they in turn would tell their children (Psalm 78:6 NIV).

Your dream is setting up someone else's dream. You are planting seeds that someone else will harvest, just as you are harvesting seeds that someone else planted.

What about a hundred years from now?

When we stand before God, He won't ask us if we have been successful. He will ask us if we've been faithful. We may think "it won't matter a hundred years from now," but faithfulness matters to God now, a hundred years from now, and in eternity.

At different points in my life, I have felt like the vision God has given me is too big for me. And that is because it is. By definition, a God-size vision or dream is beyond your ability, beyond your resources. If a vision is from God, it will require divine intervention. But I have also learned that sometimes a vision feels as if it is too big for us because it is not just for us. That is how I felt when we developed Riverview International Christian Academy. We purchased the five acres of land for $20,000. I did not have a category for a vision that big. (Honestly, I wasn't sure we had $20,000 to actually purchase the land in the first place.) But the next generation might have a vision that big. And that is who we are building it for.

It is not about us.

It is not about now.

Whatever God is doing in us here and now, He is doing for the third and fourth generation from now. The dream God has given you is the seed for something He wants to do a hundred years from now. You likely won't be around to witness it, but others are going to reap where they haven't sown because of your faithfulness.

Don't give up on your vision. If you do, you will be giving up on its future potential. Were there moments when we felt like throwing in the towel on RICA? Absolutely! Especially during the first two years. But we wouldn't have been giving up on just the four hundred and forty students who enrolled in the first years of operations. We would have been forfeiting everything God has done over the last five years and 100 years to come.

Keep dreaming God-sized visions.

It makes all the difference in the world.

It makes all the difference for eternity.

Just in case you haven't figured it out by now, "Be courageous" is not just words in a book to us. It is a call to be courageous for God in your life. It is okay to pray a hedge of protection around those you love. God is our Refuge and our Shield. But He is also a very present God who guides us and goes before us, a God who promises to prosper us. So do what you were destined to accomplish—be COURAGEOUS.

Long-Term Needs of RICA

Teachers, Staffing and Resources: Please pray for these positions to be filled. If the job description fits you, ask God how He can use you.

Science and Math Teachers: These people would teach chemistry, physics, math, or biology at a senior high level.

Various Other Instructional Staff: We are open to varying lengths of time. We need instructors for courses in language arts, reading, phonics, and entrepreneurship.

Short-Term Mission Trips

We have opportunities for short-term mission trips to Liberia and RICA that range from 10 to 14 days. We provide accommodations, meals, and local transportation at reasonable costs. These trips are designed to give you a "taste of the culture." (See more details at www. cltinternational.org, and click on mission trips.)

Typical activities for short-term mission trips include teaching in the classroom, teaching Sunday School or Vacation Bible School to children, construction work, agricultural work like planting beans or fruit trees, landscaping, teachers training, outreach to local villages/community, and workshops or seminars for pastors' continuing education.

When you come on a trip, we hope to create a safe and challenging place for you to grow in your love for Jesus. We also want you to become more aware of your own role in God's Kingdom as you build relationships with other team members. Most of our trips partner with people that are already launched into God's Kingdom revolution, so we hope that you add value to the amazing Kingdom work that is already taking place in Liberia. Lastly, we hope you experience more of God's Kingdom and that it changes you.

JAY SKINNER

Jay visited us twice in Liberia. His first visit was as we became ready to announce the groundbreaking for a college preparatory high school in Ganta, Liberia. The date was set for May 26, 2018. Jay accepted our invitation and we stayed together for a week. On the last day before returning, I asked if he has seen enough, and if God was stirring his heart in any way. Sure enough, God was at work, and upon his return home Jay committed to double his financial generosity until this day. Jay returned to RICA about a year later, saw the building almost complete and helped run a leadership and project management workshop with local government officials and staffers. Jay also became our Networking Coordinator and connected us with others who continue to support our ministry monthly.

Jay Skinner with government officials including Gompa
Mayor Amos Suah

NOTE FROM JOHN ROBERTSON

Dear Sei and Yah,

I have enjoyed such a wonderful visit to your country, community, and home. Many thanks for extending such warm hospitality to Kevin, Tim, and me these past two weeks. You have kept us safe and well, fed us deliciously, transported us regularly, and informed us of all things Liberian insight fully.

May God bless you in all your endeavors!

John Robertson

John Robertson, Tim Quiroz, and Kevin Callaway from
Santa Barbara, CA, visited from Oct. 12 – 26, 2022

RICA and CLTI Welcome Deizie Leighton Buor to Liberia
January 13 through March 7, 2023

Deizie, our older son, was two years old when we left Liberia in 1988 for Nairobi, Kenya. Fast forward to 2023 when he returned as RICA's

Soccer Coach and Director of Sports for 2 ½ months. Our students were very thrilled. Deizie and many friends in Indiana spent most of 2022 collecting and shipping soccer equipment, uniforms, cleats and other items to RICA in preparation for the launch of the team. Read what Deizie wrote:

> I can honestly say I finally feel at home. America has blessed me, raised me, and taught me many different positive and negative things. I will cherish, appreciate and share my experience the rest of my life, but I've always felt like something was missing, and it was a feeling that was unexplainable. I landed in Liberia on January 13th and have now hit almost 2 months of personal experience. It has truly been a humbling and learning experience.

> My best friend once said, "Deizie you have been Americanized." I didn't take it well because I didn't really understand what he meant. I now understand that fully. He wasn't referring to the materialistic things but that opportunity was in abundance. My 2 months have shown me the lack of opportunity in my home. Every day I have seen what we refer to in America as the struggle. People—men, women, children—are on a daily struggle looking for the means to eat, drink, sleep comfortably and provide for their families. I have seen children as young as 5 years old drawing water from wells, selling bananas, candy, and water, just trying to help their families any way they can.

> I have taken the role as Head Soccer Coach. My players commit themselves to difficult training when it's 95 degrees. 98 percent of our students and players walk or take motorbikes to school. I am extremely thrilled to join this vision in the best way I can through educating the students in sport, but also life.

Hope and opportunity are the two most important things I want to bless all students and players with. Hope is so underestimated, but it can honestly change a person's course in life. Hope is what I preach and base my whole experience here around.

Deizie with his RICA Soccer Team

Deizie with RICA Soccer Team and Visiting Team

On a short-term trip, you are potentially launching into a life-changing experience. Short-term trips are difficult, challenging, exhilarating, humbling, awe-inspiring, memorable, community-building, norm-defying, culture-shifting, and faith-building. Through a trip, you will become aware of some characteristics of God that up to now have been hidden from you. You will become more aware of who you are, and perhaps also aware of some of your own brokenness. You will become more aware of the amazing diversity that God has designed on His planet earth that reflects Him. You will become more aware of the desperate need for God's Kingdom.

Our Needs in the United States

Visionary Partners: These are friends who share in our vision, pursue our mission, and give regularly of the wealth God has given them to achieve the mission. Everyone can be a vision partner, as every gift is a sacrificial gift for God's Kingdom.

Fund Developers and Partnership and Relationship Builders: These people can be located anywhere in the United States but work to connect us with North American supporters to meet our needs for expertise, financial resources, and prayer. Each gift to RICA is used for its intended purpose as designated by the originator. This person would need to be familiar with various types of funding, networking, and developing partnerships.

Scholarships Coordinator: This U.S.-based person would match students who need funding to an individual, several individuals, or an organization that desires to sponsor or help a student at the school.

Instructional Staff Development Coordinator: This person would match a selected teacher with funding from individuals or an organization that desires to sponsor a teacher to pursue advanced studies.

If you are interested in learning more about any of these opportunities with RICA, please contact me so we can discuss the possibilities:

Dr. Sei Buor, CLTI
P. O. Box 1123
Carmel IN 46082
fsbuor1@gmail.com
sbuor@cltinternational.org
https://www.cltinternational.org

About the Author

Yah and Sei Buor

Sei's History

From an early age I was committed to pursuing an education. I continued this commitment after my life changed with the acceptance of Jesus Christ as my Lord and Savior. This eventually led me to Nairobi, Kenya, to study at Africa International University (M.Div. - Master of Divinity, 1991), the United States to study at Western Theological Seminary in Holland, Michigan (Th.M. - Master of Theology, 1996) and Loyola University in Chicago, Illinois (Ph.D. in Educational Leadership and Policy Studies, 2001).

I was a co-founder and served as the Executive Director of ULICAF from 1996 to 2015. As part of that work, I was co-founder and President of Liberia International Christian College (LICC) in Ganta, Liberia. LICC is considered by many to be the first indigenous-initiated Christian college in West Africa. Because of this experience, I am uniquely able to speak about the long and often faith-testing path God led the friends and associates of ULICAF on as they built LICC literally from the "bare ground up."

After my journey with ULICAF ended, I founded a new organization, Christian Leadership Training International to support discipleship, entrepreneurship, and education. The flagship of our efforts is Riverview International Christian Academy (RICA). We are working to build and operate what we believe will be one of the best college preparatory schools in Liberia.

Many of you already know my history because you have personally walked with me on this journey, or heard from others about my vision, or possibly because you are familiar with my writings. My first book was *No More War: Rebuilding Liberia through Faith, Determination & Education* and my second book was *Vision, Valleys & Victories: Growing Liberia International Christian College.* Other readers will be less familiar with my personal history. To all readers, I would like to give you a brief background to provide an understanding of my family and tribal background, my specific tribe's culture, and why I so much value education which eventually motivated me to start the academic institutions of LICC and RICA and see them come to fruition.

First, I believe my country needs more educated people. You should also know that for me, personally, the pursuit of education has defined my life. Education was a passion for me from a very early age.

I was born and grew up in the small village of Yarsonnoh (Riverview), Nimba County, Liberia. My first education experience was practically focused on our tribal traditions which was similar to my contemporaries. We learned how to survive in the jungle in the Poro School. We learned the basics of life—how to make clothing; how to build a shelter from branches and tree leaves; and how to find, gather, and cook food. As you can imagine, we had to learn subsistence farming from our families so we would have food to eat and could survive.

I wanted more education than that. I desperately wanted to go to elementary school. With my father's help, I was fortunate enough to be able to attend Karnwee Elementary School. This was the beginning of my western-style education. My "commute" to this school was walking 5 miles each way on dirt roads.

Through a series of fortunate circumstances, at age 10, I was able to attend the Cocopa Plantation School. This private school was a vast improvement in opportunity for me. I attended the Cocopa School to complete my grade school.

Angel in Ebony

My mother had fallen sick, so I returned to my village to help her. During this time God planted a seed by allowing me to attend a viewing of "Angel in Ebony" about the life of Samuel ("Sammy") Morris, the eldest son of a Kru tribal chief from southeastern Liberia who was captured when a neighboring clan defeated the Kru. His father could not buy him back. (Details of the story are taken from www.taylor.edu/about/Samuel-morris)

After one of numerous episodes of terrible mistreatments, Sammy Morris saw a bright light and heard the message to leave. He travelled by night through the jungle, and eventually arrived at the capital city of Monrovia. There a young boy invited Kaboo (Sammy's original name) to church where Miss Knolls, a missionary and graduate of Taylor University in Indiana, United States taught him about Paul's conversion and led him to Christ. Kaboo accepted Christ as Savior and was baptized and given the name Samuel Morris in honor of Miss Knolls' benefactor.

233

Miss Lizzie MacNeil, a missionary, encouraged him to travel to American and seek the instruction of her mentor Stephen Merritt, a former secretary to Bishop William Taylor. When he arrived in New York, Stephen Merritt contacted Thaddeus Reade, President of Taylor University, and requested to enroll Morris at the school. In 1891, Morris arrived on Taylor's campus (in Fort Wayne, Indiana).

Later President Reade said, "Samuel Morris was a divinely sent messenger of God to Taylor University. He thought he was coming over here to prepare himself for his mission to his people, but his coming was to prepare Taylor University for her mission to the whole world. All who met him were impressed with his sublime, yet simple faith in God."

The writers of the 1898 yearbook wrote, "In a little while, everyone in the school came to look on Samuel Morris with reverence; all felt that he had an unusually close and open communion with God. His insight into the scripture was perfectly marvelous."

On May 12, 1893, Samuel Morris died of pneumonia after contracting a severe cold. His death inspired his fellow students to serve as missionaries to Africa on his behalf, fulfilling his dream of one day returning to minister to his own people. Within months of his passing, his incredible story began a journey around the world continuing far into the next century and beyond with a voice that could not be silenced.

On several occasions, groups of Liberian Americans from the Sinoe County Association in the Americas (SCCA) have visited Taylor University to learn more about Samuel Morris and raise awareness of his legacy with the Liberian Community.

Although Sammy's goal was to learn enough to share the Holy Spirit with Liberia, he is often called Africa's missionary to America for his impact during his brief time in America. The missionary who converted

Sammy also emphasized the importance of education, which helped reinforce my personal desire for education.

Accepting Christ

I wasn't raised in a family that attended church, so I never really understood that there was a God who loves me and had a plan for my life. Then, at the age of 20, on my high school campus, I heard someone articulate the plan of salvation in a way that suddenly made sense to me. I came to know the saving power of Jesus Christ in high school in 1978. I met a local evangelist, Amos Miamen, on my way home from school. He was persistent in befriending me, even coming to my home! One day he asked me if I would accept Christ. I said, "Yes." I am eternally thankful to Dr. Amos Miamen and his wife Mary who shared this knowledge with me and mentored me as I grew in faith. My father was very upset at my conversion as were some of my friends from my village. For a time, my father would not speak to me or acknowledge me. I was fortunate to help many in my village, including my mother, come to know Christ.

To this day, I can recall the sense of wonder and amazement I felt as I tried to get my arms around a huge, incredible reality. The great God and Creator of the whole world actually loved and cared about Sei Buor. But as the days went by, I also learned that this same God wanted to use me. I was very young in my commitment to Christ and knew next to nothing about the Bible or the Christian life, but I had heard that I should go out and share the gospel with others.

In 1981 I started teaching at United Liberia Inland Church Academy (a high school). I learned to share the gospel under the tutelage of Rev. "Pop" Carson and served as a translator for visiting evangelists.

From that time, it gave me the hope that somehow, some way, in some measure, He would change the world through me. The truth is, God want to use every one of us as His transforming agents. But it will very well mean leaving our comfort zones and stretching our faith to attempt something we have never done before. A simple way to step forth in a new place in your life is to begin with a simple prayer: "God, I will do what you want me to do, go where you want me to go." Then stay alert for opportunities to step out in faith as the Lord opens the doors for you (see 2 Chronicles 16:9).

In 1982, I started my college education by attending African Bible College (ABC). Upon graduation, I returned to teaching and pastoring a local church. Yah and I started our family, and Yah continued her small business to help support our family.

My Educational Journey

My next educational pursuit was at an East African Seminary with an international reputation: Nairobi Evangelical Graduate School of Theology (NEGST) in Nairobi, Kenya. The institution is now part of Africa International University (AIU).

Getting there was not easy, but we eventually did get there, and I earned a Master of Divinity. During this time, both Yah and I worked small businesses to help support our family. When I graduated, civil war had broken out in Liberia. I was unable to safely return my family to Liberia and so I ended up taking a position as a pastor in Gambia with the help of World Evangelization for Christ International (WEC Int'l). While in Gambia, I began to pursue further education in the United States. I was fortunate to be accepted to Western Theological Seminary at Hope College in Holland, Michigan. Before I left for America, I wanted to return to Liberia to visit my family and to observe conditions there.

Many counseled against this, but I did manage to visit, and I did return safely.

In 1994, I flew to the United States to commence my education at Western Theological Seminary. Eventually, with the help of a local church, Christ Memorial Church, I was able to bring my family to Holland, Michigan in 1995 to live with me as I continued my education. Both Yah and I worked several jobs to support our family during our time in Holland.

When I graduated from Western Theological Seminary, the civil war was still raging, and it was considered unsafe to return. I did not know what to do. I was tired of education. Fortunately, even though it involved more education, God had a plan, and I was accepted to Loyola University near Chicago.

Ultimately, my doctorate from Loyola is the pinnacle of my educational career. I am very proud that they accepted me as a student. Loyola is a prestigious school with an international reputation for educating both Catholic and evangelical leaders. I am even happier to have done the work necessary to earn my Doctorate in Educational Leadership and Policy Studies. These were the right studies to strengthen me and give me the background I needed as I helped design the plans to develop Liberia International Christian College and now Riverview International Christian Academy.

Sei's Strong Support from Yah

Both Yah and I worked as we waited for a time when it would be safe to return to Liberia. For a while, I was a teaching assistant in the Indianapolis school district where I worked with disadvantaged children with learning disabilities. In 2005, I started full-time ministry for ULICAF as Executive Director which lasted until 2015.

If a leader is married, and if his commitment to his organization is to be strong, he or she needs the strong support of the spouse. I am fortunate that my wife has been supportive of me throughout our whole long, sometimes arduous, journey. Without her active support, this journey of leading an organization to build a college, and now a grade school, in Liberia would have been very difficult and maybe impossible. There are people I know who do not have their spouses' support. It is difficult for them to accomplish even a part of their dream. I am fortunate that Yah has stood with me through it all.

Again, if you would like to know more of my history, I would encourage you to check out my first book, *No More War: Rebuilding Liberia through Faith, Determination & Education*, and also my second book, *Vision, Valleys & Victories: Growing Liberia International Christian College*. Both are available from Amazon.

Contact Me

If you would like to contact Dr. Buor for speaking engagements, please use the following:

Dr. Sei Buor
fsbuor1@gmail.com
CLTI
P. O. Box 1123
Carmel IN 46082
sbuor@cltinternational.org
https://www.cltinternational.org

In his speaking engagements, Dr. Buor uses the stories of LICC and RICA to encourage Christians everywhere of the value of maintaining steadfast faith and adhering to Christian principles as they pursue the visions that God has laid on their own hearts.

References

Chapter 1:

Batterson, Mark. *Chase the Lion: If Your Dream Doesn't Scare You, It's Too Small.* Colorado Springs, Colorado: Multnomah, 2016.

Chapter 4:

Jennings, Janet. *The Blue and the Gray.* Madison, WI: Cantwell Printing, 1910, p. 178.

Chapter 6:

Williamson, Joe. *Finding YOUR Place in the World.* Self-published: Joe Williamson. 2010. Available from Amazon.

For more information on Sammy Morris and the statues, see www.taylor.edu/about/Samuel-morris

The three statues *The Moment of Truth*, *Heeding the Call*, and *Sharing the Word* are located north of the Rice Bell Tower behind the Modelle Metcalf Visual Arts Center at Taylor University in Upland, Indiana.

The *Moment of Truth* depicts Morris' miraculous escape after being kidnapped by a neighboring tribe. In the midst of being tortured by the tribe's Chief, Morris is seen looking upward where he sees a bright light and hears a voice from heaven telling him to flee. *Heeding the Call* shows Morris' journey to freedom through the jungle and his unwavering commitment to obey God's calling. *Sharing the Word* reveals Morris' steadfast resolve to "go into all the world and preach the Gospel" and demonstrates his Christian witness as a Taylor University student.

Chapter 17:

Maxwell, John. *The 17 Indisputable Laws of Teamwork: Embrace and Empower your Team.* Nashville, Tennessee: Thomas Nelson, 2001, pp. 4, 77.

Collins, Jim. *Good to Great: Why Some Companies Make the Leap...And Others Don't,* New York: Harper Collins Publishers, 2005, p. 14.

Chapter 22:

Buford, Bob. *Halftime: Moving from Success to Significance.* Grand Rapids, MI: Zondervan, 2008.

Powell, Colin. *It Worked for Me in Life and Leadership.* New York: Harper Perennial, 2013, p. 196.

Made in the USA
Columbia, SC
18 August 2023

21735281R00133